A BIBLICAL APPROACH

COPING

Steven Lloyd

ISBN-13: 978-1503028760

ISBN-10: 1503028763

Printed in the United States of America

Also by Steven Lloyd

Turning Points: Pivotal Moments in God's Story (2014)

Turning Points Workbook (2016)

STEVEN M. LLOYD

For

Valerie

Jim and Kari,

Julie,

Mom and Dad,

Mom and Dad Rollings

CONTENTS

ACKNOWLEDGMENTS

I would like to acknowledge the work of brother Troy Cummings and his influence on me when I was a student at the Southern California School of Evangelism in Buena Park. I do not believe a week goes by that I am not conscious of the favorable impact Troy had on me.

I would also like to thank my dear friend Don Ruhl for challenging me beyond what I would have been otherwise in matters discussed in this book. Don has been an invaluable sounding board for me ever since we were students together at S.C.S.E.

I want to thank another good friend, Tom Steed. We have engaged in countless fruitful discussions on every subject addressed in this book.

 In addition to those just mentioned, others read the book and gave me their advice: Naomi Hurst, Jerry Thompson, Wayne Jackson, Tim Nichol, Jim Lloyd, and Dave White.

In the second printing of this title, I only made a few changes—certainly not enough to qualify as a revised edition. I added a few quotes, in particular the ones that head each chapter. I also tried to tidy up the grammar. But the most significant thing I did is ask sister Joyce Smith to copy edit it. Sister Smith is a professional copy editor. When she got through with it, the manuscript looked like it had been through the Red Cross. I want to thank her for her efforts.

This is the third printing. I added two chapters in an Appendix: one on "anger," and another on "anxiety." These can be found on my website at www.turningpointsofthebible.com under "Books."

INTRODUCTION

I feel like Amos, a prophet of old, who identified himself by writing, "I was no prophet, neither was I a prophet's son; but I was a herdsman, and a dresser of sycamore-trees" (Amos 7:14). I am no psychologist, neither am I a psychologist's son. I was schooled in the Scriptures. I have preached the gospel since 1980 and was involved in training others to do the same for thirteen of those years.

The primary impetus for this book is the distinct impression so many professed Christians have made on me concerning their attitude toward the Bible, namely, their implicit rejection of the sufficiency of the Bible in helping them with their emotional-mental-spiritual problems.

This book is based on two premises. The first is that the Bible is inspired of God and profitable for teaching, reproof, correction, and instruction that the man of God may be complete, furnished completely unto every good work (2 Timothy 3:16-

17). The second is that God has granted to us all things that pertain to life and godliness through a knowledge of His Son (2 Peter 1:3).

It is not a "self-help" book because I do not believe the answer is in us just waiting to be discovered upon further reflection. The answers are with God. That is why God provides man with His written word.

Self-help books tell us about things that have pragmatically helped some—sometimes. This book begins with the Word of God as the divine standard and strives to move the reader to accept certain basic truths in order to effectively cope with the problems life throws our way. Its solutions work, and from that standpoint, it is pragmatic.

I began developing this material with Tom Steed. We listed the various issues common among the people that came to us for help. I then asked myself the question, "What does God's Word say concerning these issues?" In the span of about 3 years, this book took shape.

I know that some may read this book and be disappointed that it is not centered exclusively on their particular problem, like alcoholism, abuse, pornography. But, in principle, it addresses all of them.

The worksheets that follow each chapter are designed to help the reader see the connection between whatever it is he or she faces and what the Bible has to say concerning it.

The principles addressed in this book are crucial for the well being of all people. We sometimes deceive ourselves into believing that some of "us" don't need the same advice that "others" need. We all need to know these principles and how they relate to us; if not to help us out of trouble, then to prevent us from getting into unnecessary trouble, or to help others.

The first chapter is the longest. It lays a foundation for everything else that is said. It deals with the primary purpose of life. The second chapter addresses the problem. The Bible calls it sin. The third chapter focuses on the issue of faith. When we face trouble, we all place our faith in someone or something. God is the only one worthy of our trust. The Fourth Chapter draws our attention to the Word of God as the answer book for the troubles that ail us. Chapter Five is designed to show us how we can insure lasting success in coping with the problems we face. The next three chapters go together. They stress the importance of approaching the issues of life with the proper attitude of humility, of holding ourselves accountable for the decisions we make, and of being honest in assessing ourselves. These are high hurdles to jump. Chapter Nine focuses on the subject of change. Some people are afraid of change, even change for the good. Chapter Ten affirms that God stands ready to forgive us when we change. Abstinence is the subject of Chapter Eleven. There are some things we cannot afford to engage in, even in moderation. Our need for the support and encouragement the church provides is the subject of Chapter Twelve. Learning to remain current with the issues we face is the focus of Chapter Thirteen. The problem of loneliness is dealt with in Chapter Fourteen. Being able to attach value to the trials and temptations of life closes out the book.

I submit this work with the hope that it will call all of us back to God and His Word for our solutions to the issues of life.

1

PURPOSE

If there is some end of the things we do...will not knowledge of it, have a great influence on life? Shall we not, like archers who have a mark to aim at, be more likely to hit upon what we should? If so, we must try, in outline at least, to determine what it is. —Aristotle

Aristotle was right. If there is "some end of the things we do," meaning some supreme purpose for which we live, knowledge of that end will have a great influence on life. Some, of course, deny there is any such supreme purpose. Others argue that each person's purpose is different.

Have the circumstances of your life ever provoked you to ask the question, "Why am I here?" Perhaps your questions have been the more desperate kind like, "Why was I ever born?" or "Is this all there is to life?" You are not alone.

The wisest man who ever lived described life as monotonous

and meaningless.

> One generation passes away, and another generation comes;
>> But the earth abides forever.
> The sun also rises, and the sun goes down,
>> And hastens to the place where it arose.
> The wind goes toward the south,
>> And turns around to the north;
>> The wind whirls about continually,
>> And comes again on its circuit.
> All the rivers run into the sea,
>> Yet the sea is not full;
>> To the place from which the rivers come,
>> There they return again
> All things are full of labor; man cannot express it (Ecclesiastes 1:4-8).

The Book of Ecclesiastes rehearses Solomon's quest for the truly worthwhile in life (2:3ff). And the corresponding question that echoes throughout the book is, "What profit has a man from all his labor in which he toils under the sun?"

We might express it in this way today: We go to bed late, we get up early, we go to work, we drive home, eat and go to bed, to get up early, to go to work, to come home, ad nausea. And, as if that were not enough, we are plagued with making ends meet financially, fighting off the latest virus, hoping to avoid some dreaded disease, mistreated at work and abused at home, and then we die. Every aspect of life seems vain. It is like striving after the wind.

A man named Job was driven to ponder the significance of life after losing his livestock to marauders, his children to murderers, and his health to Satan. All that was left to him was the breath of life and a wife who counseled him to renounce God and die. Job was a man in a desperate situation.

He made statements like, "May the day perish on which I was born, and the night in which it was said, 'A male child is conceived'" (Job 3:3). And he asked questions like:

Why did I not die at birth?
Why did I not perish when I came from the womb?
Why did the knees receive me?
Or why the breasts, that I should nurse? (3:11-12).

Why is light given to him who is in misery,
And life to the bitter of soul,
Who long for death, but it does not come,
And search for it more than hidden treasures;
Who rejoice exceedingly,
And are glad when they can find the grave? (3:20-22).

What value is there in such misery and misfortune?

When Jesus walked this earth he passed by a man who was blind from birth. His disciples asked Him, "Rabbi, who sinned, this man, or his parents?" (John 9:1-2). Their inquiry assumed that sin was the direct cause of this man's blindness. Jesus corrected their misinformed notion by saying, "Neither did this man sin, nor his parents: but that the works of God should be made manifest in him" (9:3).

Job's fair-weather friends believed that Job must have done some despicably wicked thing to have fallen victim to the calamities described in the first two chapters of Job, and the disciples of our Lord believed that the blindness of the man in John 9 was the direct result of sin—either his or his parents. Both parties were wrong. So how do we make sense out of life and the varying circumstances in which we find ourselves?

7

THE PURPOSE OF LIFE

The Scriptures make it clear that the purpose of all creation is to glorify God. To glorify God is to magnify Him. In particular, the God we are to glorify is the One who reveals Himself to us through the Scriptures and through nature.

Consider these passages:

- Jehovah described Israel as a people He created for His glory (Isaiah 43:7).

- The heavens declare the glory of God;
  And the firmament shows his handiwork (Psalm 19:1).

- Jesus said, "Let your light so shine before men, that they may see your good works and glorify your Father in heaven" (Matthew 5:16).

- Or do you not know that your body is the temple of the Holy Spirit who is in you, whom you have from God, and you are not your own? For you were bought at a price; therefore glorify God in your body and in your spirit which are God's (1 Corinthians 6:19-20).

- Peter wrote that if a man is going to speak, let him speak the oracles of God; if he is going to minister, let him do so in the strength which God supplies "that in all things God may be glorified through Jesus Christ, to whom belongs the glory and the dominion forever and ever. Amen." (1 Peter 4:11)

MISSING THE MARK

My father would get upset with me when I used his tools for some purpose other than the purpose for which they were designed. I might use a pipe wrench as a hammer, or a screwdriver as a chisel. His frustration was well founded in that the tool I misused was usually ruined or significantly altered so that it was of no use to him when he needed it.

In like manner, Christians were created in Christ Jesus for good works (Ephesians 2:8-10), and those good works will be the cause of others glorifying God (Matthew 5:16). If we do not live our lives with respect for the purpose for which we were created, we too will be of little use to our Father. In fact, living for any other purpose will bring upon us dire consequences.

In the introduction of Paul's letter to the saints in Rome, he writes of those who, knowing God, "…glorified him not as God, neither gave thanks," and he tells us that "they became vain in their reasonings and their senseless heart was darkened" (Romans 1:21). How could anyone legitimately expect to successfully cope with the conflicts of life if they become vain in their reasonings and their senseless hearts are darkened?

Are you beginning to see how vital a clear perspective on the purpose of life is in relationship to coping with problems? Not having a clear vision of the reason for our existence may very well be one of the biggest problems of all.

GLORIFYING GOD

Let's say John Doe is seeking help. John has a serious problem, but doesn't know what to do. In his efforts to cope he turns to drugs and alcohol. Then, he seeks counsel from a leader he respects in the church who reminds him of several biblical principles, one of which is that he exists for the purpose of glorifying God. John says, "I know that! But it hasn't helped."

What John may fail to see is the connection between his problems and the purpose of life.

John may need help seeing the implications of such a purpose-driven life. It may be that John Doe doesn't have a clear picture of who God is because he hasn't spent the necessary time reading and meditating on what God has revealed about Himself. It may also be the case that John has simply chosen to value some things as more important.

GOD

What is your concept of God? From where has your concept of Him come? Do your problems influence how you think about God? For example, many people transfer their attitudes concerning their earthly father to the heavenly Father. If their earthly father was stern and unloving, then their view of God is sometimes the same.

All correct thinking about God begins with the Scriptures. The Scriptures inform us that God is incomparable in nature.

- To whom then will you liken Me, Or to whom shall I be equal? says the Holy One (Isaiah 40:25).

- I am the Lord, that is My name; And My glory I will not give to another, Nor my praise to graven images (Isaiah 42:8).

- Before Me there was no God formed (Isaiah 43:10).

- I am the Lord, and there is no other; there is no God besides Me. I will gird you, though you have not known Me, that they may know from the rising of the sun to its setting that there is none besides Me. I am the Lord, and there is no other; I form the light and create darkness, I make peace and create calamity; I, the Lord, do all these things (Isaiah 45:5-7).

- God, who made the world and everything in it, since He is Lord of heaven and earth, does not dwell in temples made with hands. Nor is He worshiped with men's hands, as though He needed anything, since he gives to all life, breath, and all things. And he has made from one blood every nation of men to dwell on all the face of the earth, and has determined their pre-appointed times and the boundaries of their habitation, so that they should seek the Lord, in the hope that they might grope for Him and find Him, though He is not far from each one of us; for in Him we live and move and have our being, as also some of your own poets have said, "For we are also His offspring (Acts 17:24-29).

Unless we continually saturate our minds with a knowledge of the true and living God, we are not going to cope with our problems successfully because coping depends largely on how we relate to God. And how can we relate to God properly without a sufficient knowledge of Him?

> Once you become aware that the main business that you are here for is to know God, most of life's problems fall into place of their own accord. —J. I. Packer

Now, back to my question: What is the connection between John Doe's problem and the purpose of life? Or, on a personal note, what does the purpose of life have to do with our problems?

God is able to use the various trials and troubles we face to see where our faith is (1 Peter 1:3). When we are faced with trouble, God is watching to see where we turn for help. Some turn to drugs and alcohol, like John Doe; others to sex, music, etc. A few turn to God. So, the problems we face can either become the means by which we fall or they can be a springboard to spiritual growth and maturity.

In the case of Job, not all of the questions posed by him or his "friends" were ever answered in the Book. The essence of God's message to Job was that God is in control, and what Job needed to do was to place his confidence in God. Satan accused Job of serving God because God had built a wall of protection around Job, blessed the work of his hands, and increased his wealth (1:9-10). So, God permitted all of these things to be taken from Job. Was God still worthy of Job's worship and service? Yes, God was still worthy because He is the Creator and we are his creatures, designed for the purpose of glorifying Him, even in the face of trials, trouble, and death. When we glorify God, even in the pit of despair, we are acknowledging that God is not the cause of our trouble.

In the days of Joshua, about 36 Israelites were killed in the siege against Ai. Joshua and the leaders of Israel turned to God and questioned Him concerning their loss.

> Alas, Lord God, why have You brought this people over the Jordan at all - to deliver us into the hand of the Amorites, to destroy us? Oh, that we had been content, and dwelt on the other side of the Jordan!" (Joshua 7:7).

They blamed God for the loss of those 36 men, when in reality sin had hidden itself in the tent of a thief named Achan.

During their siege against Jericho, Achan had stolen some things God told them to destroy, "...a beautiful Babylonian garment, two hundred shekels of silver, and a wedge of gold weighing fifty shekels..." (7:21). Joshua said to Achan, "...give glory to the Lord God of Israel, and make confession to Him, and tell me now what you have done; do not hide it from me" (7:19).

And Achan said, "I coveted them and took them. And there they are, hidden in the earth in the midst of my tent, with the silver under it" (7:21).

How did Achan's confession of sin glorify God? His confession put the spotlight on the real cause of Israel's trouble, and, at the same time, acquitted God.

How can God be glorified by your life? The same way He has always been glorified: by faithful obedience to His will. In so doing, our lives prove that such a life is good and acceptable and perfect (Romans 12:2).

Obedience is equated with good works, for which we have been created (Ephesians 2:10). Those good works spring forth from a heart full of faith in God. Jesus provides for us the supreme example of One who glorified God through His life. Jesus Himself affirmed: "He (God) hath not left me alone; for I do always the things that are pleasing to him" (John 8:29).

STUMBLING BLOCKS

A common problem for many of us is being so wrapped up in gratifying our own wants and needs that we forget it is God we are to serve. We become so problem-oriented that we take our eyes off God, and lose our focus on the very purpose for our existence.

When our focus is on the cares and riches and pleasures of life, God's Word is choked out and no fruit in our life is brought to perfection (Luke 8:14). The will of God is stifled by our pursuit of the things of the world. You know, "The one with the most toys wins!"

Luke records a conversation between Jesus and a certain ruler (Luke 18:18-20). Jesus referred the man to the Law. The man responded by saying, "All these things have I kept from my youth." When Jesus heard it, He said, "You still lack one thing. Sell all that you have and distribute to the poor, and you will have treasure in heaven; and come, follow Me" (18:22).

Do you remember how the man reacted? "He became exceeding sorrowful; for he was very rich" (18:23). As far as this man was concerned, the ultimate end of life was to maintain his wealth. This rich ruler was asked to choose between purposes, but he could not see past his riches. Jesus once said, "…a man's life consists not in the abundance of the things which he possesses" (Luke 12:15).

Another stumbling block to glorifying God is the belief that happiness is the highest goal to be obtained. Aristotle identifies happiness as the supreme end to which each of us lives. Ironically, when happiness becomes our goal of goals, we become self-oriented and our pursuit ends up being very counter-productive. This is not to say that happiness is not important or that it is wrong to be happy. Happiness is a by-product of a higher goal— living a life that glorifies God.

Another factor that figures into this matter is attitude. A person may know what his purpose is, and understand it, and yet live in such a way that God is not glorified.

What hindrances to honoring and glorifying God do you find in your life? Are they similar to the ones listed above?

RESOLUTIONS

Knowing that your ultimate purpose in life is to bring glory to God, resolve:

- to be more concerned about God's reputation than your own.

- to work in such a way that you bring glory to Him and not attention to yourself.

- not to frustrate God's will for your life by establishing your own selfish purposes contrary to His plan for your life.

- not to act in such a way as to detract from the glory that is rightfully His.

- to serve the Lord with your whole house (Joshua 24:15).

THINGS TO CONSIDER

Keeping in mind the fact that the ultimate purpose in life is to glorify God, consider how this might alter the way you deal with the problems you are presently facing. What difference would this make in your life today?

For example, how would this alter the way husbands and wives resolve their conflicts? Would a husband or wife resort to spiteful, hateful tactics designed to hurt one another remembering this important truth? Imagine how circumstances might be different if each one tried to resolve their conflicts in a way that honored God.

Consider how this might revolutionize every area of your life. Knowing that the reason for your existence is to glorify God, you should want to do always those things that are pleasing to Him (John 8:29).

The only thing that stands between our knowledge of these truths and living to fulfill our purpose is a decision. We must consciously choose to love the Lord with all our heart, and all our soul, and with all of our mind (Matthew 22:37). Otherwise, we will not want to fulfill our purpose with the wholeheartedness required to succeed.

****

Alexander the Great ascended to the throne at 20 years of age. Aristotle was his boyhood teacher. His favorite book was the *Iliad* (by Homer). In fact, he saw himself as a second Achilles (a Greek demi-god). His ultimate goal was world-domination under one government, as one people and one culture. So fierce and effective was his military prowess that the Lord described him prophetically as being "…like a leopard which had on its back four wings of a bird. The beast also had four heads and dominion was given to it" (Daniel 7:6). In less than 14 years, Alexander had achieved his goal. Greece ruled the world.

In the spring of 323 B.C., he reached Babylon, but in June a fever struck and he grew so weak that he couldn't even speak. He could only signal through his eyelids. On June 13, 323 B.C., not yet 33, Alexander died.

Jesus asks us, "For what is a man profited if he gains the whole world, and loses his own soul? Or what will a man give in exchange for his soul?" (Matthew 16:26).

Ivan Ilyich, the character of one of Leo Tolstoy's books, was a man who busied himself so much with his career as high court judge that he never gave the inevitability of his dying a passing thought. But one day death presented itself to him and he was not prepared. Countless thousands in our world today are living their lives without thought that one day death will claim them too. They are living their lives without giving it a passing thought.

I asked my grandfather if he had ever contemplated the thought of life after death, or heaven and hell, or if he had ever pursued God. I find it hard to believe that anyone could say "No," but he did. If he was telling me the truth, even though he had suffered several paralyzing strokes in his lifetime, he never did give thought to the things discussed in this chapter. He died without giving it much further thought.

Socrates said the unexamined life was not worth living.

PURPOSE WORKSHEET

The inner circle with the question mark below represents the primary end and purpose around which people plan their lives. From the list of goals provided, which would accurately represent what you have placed in the center of your life?

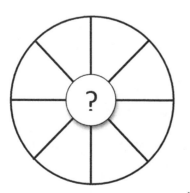

Pleasure

Money

Health

Honor, Fame, Glory

Power

Peace, Contentment

Helping Others

Virtue

Wisdom

Notice that none of the above items are inherently evil, but, in fact, could even be considered good. But the one we place in the center could drastically alter how effectively we cope with problems.

Solomon, the wise king of old, went in search of what was truly worthwhile in life (Ecclesiastes 2:3), and after giving all of them a try he concluded that they were vain and like striving after the wind. Here is what he said:

> Fear God and keep His commandments, For this is the whole duty of man. For God will bring every work into judgment, Including every secret thing, Whether it is good or whether it is evil (Ecclesiastes 12:13-14).

Far too often, we get so wrapped up in our own problems, and in trying to meet our own needs and wants, that we forget it is God we are to serve. As a result, God is shoved into the back seat or is left out of the picture altogether.

CONSIDER THESE PASSAGES:

1. Matthew 5:16

2. 1 Corinthians 6:19-20

3. 1 Corinthians 10:31

THINK ABOUT IT

1. What is the primary goal in your life?

2. What does it mean to glorify God?

3. Identify the conflict(s) or issue(s) in your life.

4. Remembering that glorifying God is the primary purpose in life, what would you do differently?

5. How would glorifying God alter your decision-making process?

6. How have you been adversely affected by not seeking to glorify God - by not making it your primary purpose in life?

7. What attitudes or purposes might stand in the way of the purpose for which God created us?

From the Scriptures

1. Read 1 Samuel 17

   a. What was David's purpose in fighting Goliath?

   b. What was it that gave David the courage to fight the giant?

2. Read Daniel 4

   a. What was Nebuchadnezzar's primary purpose in life?

   b. How did God humble him?

3. How did Jesus glorify God?

   a. John 8:29

   b. John 17:4

4. How did the Gentiles fail to glorify God? Romans 1:18-23

Read and Meditate

1. Psalm 24

2. Psalm 29

STEVEN M. LLOYD

2

THE PROBLEM

The very notion of sin is unpalatable to the modern mind. As a result, many
of the brightest Western Thinkers have constructed a great myth to avoid
facing the truth about sin and guilt. And ironically, this myth, more than
anything else, has wrought unimaginable havoc and misery into this century.
—Charles Colson

Their relationship was a roller coaster ride. John would treat
Sue fine one minute and like dirt the next. It was far from
the picture painted by Paul of husbands loving their wives
(Eph. 5:22-33).

Sue was very hurt by John's lack of respect for her, and the
longer she put up with it the more upset she got. Her friends
sided with her in the matter, taking up the offense for her, and
expressing their outrage at the way she was being treated. All it
did was convert Sue's anger to bitterness.

This condition went unresolved for years. Sue, finally fed up the situation, found a more understanding man to sympathize with her—a man that would listen and show he cared. She finally chose the path many people take in similar circumstances. She gave herself to this other man in ways that should be reserved for her husband.

We all have certain needs. The Bible reduces man's list of needs to at least the following: food, drink and clothing (Matt. 6:25, 31-32; 1 Tim. 6:6-10), companionship (Gen. 2:18) and the Word of God (Job 23:12). Of course, there are also perceived needs—things we want so much that we perceive them as needs. Sometimes these perceived needs lead to murmuring and complaining about our current provisions.

When our needs (real or perceived) are not met we hurt. If we do not deal with the hurt in a responsible way, it can fester into anger and ultimately bitterness. How we handle our anger and bitterness will make the difference between seeking effective solutions and creating additional problems. Unfortunately, most people try to satisfy their needs in ways other than the way prescribed by God. So, rather than dealing effectively with the initial problem, we compound it by adding sin to sin.

It is my personal opinion that man's efforts to cope with problems have been abysmal. And to compound matters, those who have not yet learned to manage their own lives freely give their useless advice and opinions concerning everyone else's problems. We have here a classic case of the blind leading the blind; and both will fall into the pit (Matt. 15:14).

THE PROBLEM ACCORDING TO MAN
Some problems have, for too long, been misdiagnosed. They have

been misdiagnosed because we went to the wrong source for help. The wrong source was the world and the world has misdiagnosed the problem because it views man as a strictly material being, a being without a spirit or mind.

At the center of our confusion is the fact that we do not want to categorize our problems as "sin." And yet, if we do not acknowledge that the problems we face are related to sin, we will be powerless to cope effectively with them. Because we do not want to "stigmatize" our problems as sin, we take our evils and failings to the psychologist and not to God.

I once knew a woman who abandoned Christianity for secular psychology. She abandoned Christianity because she abhorred the doctrine of hell. In her own words, she said, "I've traded God in for psychology."

> The language of codependency is the language of physical disease and health. At times one wonders if a rapist is any more responsible for his own actions than a cancer patient is responsible for his or her disease. Codependents have a disease or an addiction; never will you hear of personal sin and repentance. In recovery groups people are now "healing," "recovering," or "addicted." They have experienced 'pain,' or "woundings." Notice, in this sort of language, they have not themselves done anything for which they are responsible. Even the addiction has an excuse. Innate, biological "needs" leave us 'sick' if they are neglected, and "toxic parents" are part of the problem." — Edward Welch

The basic presupposition of modern-day secular counseling is that man is essentially good and that if he searches his heart long enough, he will find the solutions to his problems. Solutions are found in one's self, not outside one's self, so we are told. Man is not in need of redemption or forgiveness, but enlightenment. All we need to do is learn to love ourselves. Virtually everything promoted in this kind of literature relegates man's problems to the realm of physical disease and health.

Consider these statements from some of the more popular self-help books:

> Total self-love and acceptance is the only foundation for happiness and the love of others (Bradshaw 1988, ix).

> We are recovering through loving and focusing on ourselves (Workbook. 1989, p. 133).

> We can cherish ourselves and our lives. We can nurture ourselves and love ourselves. We can accept our wonderful selves, with all our foolish faults, foibles, strong points, weak points, feelings, thoughts and everything else. It's the best thing we've got going for us. It's who we are, and who we were meant to be and it's not a mistake. We are the greatest thing that will ever happen to us. Believe it. It makes life much easier (Beattie, p.113).

In some corners of today's church there are accomplices to the problem—people who are promoting the substitution of psychology for divine revelation. Some counselors trust more in their secular training in psychology than in the Word of God. Consequently, they unwittingly promote some non-biblical, even anti-biblical, ideas. One such man has gone so far as to affirm that the headship of a man in the home has leads to incest. Because women are inclined to view their husbands in the same vein they view their fathers, they are less inclined toward intimacy, so the husband turns to the daughter for intimacy.

Most of our problems are problems of living. I am not denying that there are adverse chemical reactions that occur in our bodies that can affect how we feel. I am simply affirming that any problem that could be treated by today's psychologist could be better treated by turning to God and His Word.

THE PROBLEM ACCORDING TO GOD

God has a standard by which all men are to live. When we fail to live according to that standard, we sin. To sin is to miss the mark, much like an archer who aims at the bull's eye and lets his arrow fly... but misses. We may miss the mark by choice or by ignorance, but we have nevertheless missed the mark. Paul wrote, "...all have sinned and fall short of the glory of God" (Romans 3:23).

Sin is defined in the Scriptures as:

• that which is not of faith (Romans 14:23)

• knowing to do good and not doing it (James 4:17)

• lawlessness (1 John 3:4)

• unrighteousness (1 John 5:17; Romans 1:18)

Sin is at the heart of many of our problems, but we have been convinced that sin is some throwback idea of an earlier uninformed era of time. When people visit the office of some psychologists today they hear the same message the false prophets of old used to deliver. These counselors heal the hurt of people slightly by saying, "Peace, peace," when there is no peace (Jeremiah 6:14).

In Jeremiah's day, God said that Judah had committed two

25

evils: "they have forsaken Me, the fountain of living waters, and hewn themselves cisterns—broken cisterns, that can hold no water" (Jeremiah 2:13). Rather than place their confidence in God, they turned to other nations and gods (who are no gods) for help. Many in our day turn from the clean and clear flowing water of God to broken cisterns that can hold no water, just like the woman who traded God in for psychology.

Why do people turn away from God? Perhaps because He is too often viewed as a cosmic killjoy; as someone Who does not permit us to experience any enjoyment in life. "Why else would there be so many commands to restrict us from so many pleasures?" we think to ourselves.

What God requires of us is for our own benefit. Consequently, if we disobey Him or if we are ignorant of His statutes and act accordingly, we are not going to experience the abundant life promised to us by the Lord Jesus Christ (John 10:10). God's desire for all men is that they come to a knowledge of the truth and live the abundant life. Man's chief end is to glorify God and to enjoy Him forever. The Lord's prescription for happiness is explicitly outlined in the Sermon on the Mount (Matthew 5:1-12). So, we need to realize that God is not withholding some good thing from us. He wants us to avoid all evil; to let Him bless our lives with good and perfect gifts (Jas. 1:17).

TEMPTATION
Why is it that sin has such a powerful hold on us? Is it because we are willing to try anything once to see if we are missing out on some good thing? This was certainly the case in the Garden of

Eden (Genesis 3:1-6). The serpent said to Eve, "Has God indeed said, 'You shall not eat of every tree of the garden'?"

And the woman said, "We may eat the fruit of the trees of the garden; but of the fruit of the tree which is in the midst of the garden, God has said, 'You shall not eat it, nor shall you touch it, lest you die.'"

The serpent said, "You will not surely die. For God knows that in the day you eat of it your eyes will be opened, and you will be like God, knowing good and evil."

"So when the woman saw that the tree was good for food, that it was pleasant to the eyes, and a tree desirable to make one wise, she took of its fruit and ate. She also gave to her husband with her, and he ate."

Eve was led to believe that God was withholding some good thing from her in forbidding her to eat of the tree of the knowledge of good and evil.

Just imagine the kind of trouble we could get ourselves into if we adopt the attitude that we are willing to try anything once for fear that we might be missing out on some good thing. For example, imagine deciding that one partner in marriage may be restricting us from experiencing some good thing. How do we know whether or not we are robbing ourselves of some pleasure or good by being with only one spouse all our life? If I were to adopt such a philosophy and committed adultery to see if God was withholding some good thing from me, consider the effect that would have on my children, my brethren in Christ, my parents, me, God. Not to mention jeopardizing the soul of the one with which I committed adultery.

We must trust that He knows what is best for us. Eve thought that God was withholding some good thing from her, but she learned that she was wrong. If I transgress God's will believing He is withholding some good thing from me, I will learn the same lesson. Have you ever done something prohibited by God believing that some pleasure or good thing was being withheld from you? Solomon asked the question, "For who knows what is good for man in life, all the days of his vain life which he passes like a shadow?" (Ecclesiastes 6:12). God knows!

The consequences of sin include alienation (Eph 4:18; Isa. 59:1, 2), guilt (Romans 2:15, our conscience accusing or excusing us), trouble (Proverbs 13:15), and death (Romans 6:23).

Consider these well thought out words from J. W. McGarvey:

I wonder if any of us has ever realized what it is to commit sin. I believe that I would esteem above every other gift that could be bestowed upon me as a preacher, the power to adequately conceive what sin is, and to adequately set it before the people. A number of times in my ministrations, I have prepared sermons designed to set forth the enormity of sin; but I have every time felt that I made a failure. I found, I thought, two causes of the failure: first, a want of realization in my own soul of the enormity of it; and second, inability to gather up such words and such figures of speech as would, with anything like adequacy, set it forth before my hearers. The pleasures of sin have blinded our eyes to its enormity. So I have come to the conclusion, after a great deal of reflection, and a great deal of mental effort, that about the only correct gauge we have with which to measure the enormity or heinousness of sin, is the punishment that 'God has decreed against it. God is infinite in all his attributes; infinite in mercy, in love, in compassion; and when we find the punishment that such a God as this was constrained, by the justice that also characterizes him, to enact against sin, I think we shall be better able to form an idea of its enormity than we can from any other view of the matter (McGarvey 1975, p.16, 17).

On minimizing sin, Sheldon VanAuken writes,

...according to some of the deepest Christian thinkers, the sense of sin has never in the 20 centuries of Christendom been at such a low ebb, partly because of psychiatric 'explaining away' (Varghese 1984, p. 305, 306).

Addressing man's unwillingness to call sin "sin," Jack Cottrell argues,

Of course he (modern man) recognizes that the world is filled with evils, failures, social ills, and conflicts of all kinds; but he just does not want to think of them as sin. This is because sin connotes a wrongdoing for which one is responsible before God, and modern man does not want to see himself in this light. He will take his evil and his failures to sociologists and psychologists, but not to God (Cottrell 1987, p. 10).

The apostle John identifies the root causes of all our problems. He writes,

For all that is in the world—the lust of the flesh, the lust of the eyes, and the pride of life—is not of the Father but is of the world. And the world is passing away, and the lust of it; but he who does the will of God abides forever" (1 John 2:16-17).

May God grant us the eyes to see that the pleasures of sin last only for a season (Hebrews 11:25).

Sin truly is at the root of man's conflicts. And until we are ready to acknowledge that, we will not be ready to escape the wickedness that ravages our lives.

COPING AS VICTIM

It may be the case that you were the victim of someone else's wickedness and that you have pointed an accusing finger at the perpetrator to excuse yourself for practicing some other evil thing. If we believe that your sinful behavior is under someone else's control, two things will follow:

- you will never take the necessary steps required to bring about healthy living;

- you will forever be frustrated believing that the problem lies with someone else—that we are powerless to change our circumstances or the quality of our life.

It may very well be the case that someone else's wrong behavior toward us has adversely influenced us, but ultimately we are the ones making the choices concerning our behavior.

For example, it may be that our father was a drunkard, that we took up drinking, and that we consequently justifying our drinking problem due of our father's influence on us. While it is true that the influence was evil and perhaps even powerful, we are the ones who decide to drink or not to drink. We are ultimately responsible. We become partners in crime.

I happened across a woman who tried to excuse her two daughters' lesbianism because their father raped them. What their father did was an abominable thing, but not all women who are raped by their fathers turn to homosexuality—and not all who practice lesbianism were raped. It is a choice they make; an unwise choice because it is as detestable in the sight of God as the crime committed against them.

Notice how all of this ties in with the purpose of life. Drunkenness does not glorify God. Consequently, even though we have been influenced by someone else's evil behavior, if we want to glorify God we will not drink. We will not participate in anything that would hinder that great purpose.

We do not cope with our problems effectively because we would rather not focus on our part in the matter. But when we sin we become partners in crime. It will not do to point an accusing finger at everyone else to excuse our part in the deed. We must learn to focus on our part and to care for it first. As Jesus our Lord put it, "First remove the plank from your own eye, and then you will see clearly to remove the speck out of your brother's eye" (Matthew 7:5).

What we need to do is learn how to hate every evil way, which comes through meditating on God's Word (which we will discuss in detail in Chapter Five). One of the Psalmists write:

I have restrained my feet from every evil way,

That I may keep Your word. Through Your precepts I get understanding;

Therefore I hate every false way (Psalm 119:101, 104).

Our problems should not be viewed through the spectacles of secular psychologists, but rather through the penetrating light of God's Word. Then our problems will be shown for what they really are.

PROBLEM WORKSHEET

In order to face a problem that has made life unmanageable, we must acknowledge that we have sinned (Romans 3:23). Some modern-day psychologists may want to relegate sinful behavior to what is natural, and being natural they seek to excuse it. How does the Bible define sin?

1. Romans 14:23

2. James 4:17

3. 1 John 3:4

4. 1 John 5:17; Romans 1:18

And the wages of sin is death (Romans 6:23).

Sin is at the root of many of man's problems (if not somehow related to all of them). And until we are ready to acknowledge this, we are not ready to begin coping with the ravages of wickedness. It may be that we were victims of someone else's wickedness, and that we pointed an accusing finger at them in order to excuse the wickedness we practice. (It is not uncommon for those who were victims of sexual crimes as children, to be caught up, and perhaps addicted to, sexual crimes themselves.)

If we believe that the problem lies outside ourselves, we will never take the necessary step(s) required to bring about healthy living and we will forever be frustrated believing that the problem lies with someone else's behavior, whom we are powerless to change.

Think About It

1. In what way is sin related to your problem? Or how has sin

created a problem for you?

2. In what way(s) have you been an accomplice in advancing the problem?

3. In what ways have you sought to excuse your behavior by assigning the blame to someone else?

Examples from the Scriptures

1. Read Genesis 3

    a. Identify the sin of Adam and of Eve.

    b. When confronted with their sin, what did Adam say? What did Eve say?

    c. How was their response typical of how people today respond when confronted with their sins?

2. Read 2 Samuel 11-12

    a. Identify the sin(s) of David.

    b. How did he try to "cover up" his transgression?

    c. What did Nathan, the prophet, do to get David to pass judgment on himself?

    d. How did David respond? (2 Samuel 12:13)

Read and Meditate

1. Psalm 32

2. Psalm 51 (Take note of the historical reference given just before vs 1)

3. How did David describe the effects of hiding his sin?

4. What benefits or blessings belong to the one who acknowledges his sin before God?

5. List what you learn about God and His nature or character from these two Psalms.

3

FAITH

The righteous shall live by faith. —Habakkuk

Steve Allen scripted and hosted a series of television programs in which actors feigned being some notable character in history. One actor might play the part of famous philosopher, another a great composer, and still another a revolutionary. They would engage in a round-table discussion on some great idea like justice, or happiness, or such like.

Philosopher Peter Kreeft engages in this same kind of dialogue in his book *Between Heaven and Hell*. In it he imagines a dialogue between C. S. Lewis, John F. Kennedy and Aldous Huxley (all of whom died within hours of each other) to investigate the claims of Christ.

Along these same lines, I want you to imagine that you are seated at a table with Sigmund Freud, Abraham Maslow, some modern-day psychotherapist, and Jesus Christ. The subject matter in this imagined conversation centers around a problem of living that you take very seriously. To which one of these guests would you most likely address your questions in an effort to solve your problem? Whose advice would you value the most?

If you were living by faith in God you would say, "Jesus Christ," who is prophetically described by Isaiah as the "Wonderful Counselor" (Isa 9:6). And yet, by virtue of the time spent reading the myriads of self-help books and observing who people actually turn to for help, have we not, practically speaking, chosen the secular psychologists of our time over the Lord?

> Only psychology, we are told, can divine our secret motivations and reveal the elusive 'why' of the strange human animal. The rules of discovery require professional interpretation. Just as the clergy once mediated between man and his soul, so the psychiatric and psychological profession must now interpret the mind for man. — Martin L. Gross

I have heard people who profess belief in God say that they did not find "real" solutions to their problems until they read such-and-such a book; or until they went to some secular support group.

I once met a Christian woman who had been in and out of various psychiatric wards most of her adult life. She fell away years prior to our association, but I met her when she decided to give God one more chance. She became semi-active in the church for several months but eventually gave up on God, telling me she decided to trade God in for psychology. How effective can any counseling be that is divorced from God and void of the knowledge found in His Word?

The "self-help" books are called such for good reason. The authors of these books believe that the answers to your questions and the solutions to your problems can be found deep within you —if you look long and hard enough. But the notion that we are able to solve our own problems independent from God is as far from the truth as you can get.

Please consider these passages:

- There is a way that seems right to a man,
  But the end is the way of death (Proverbs 14:12).
- He who trusts in his own heart is a fool,
  But whoever walks wisely will be delivered (Proverbs 28:26).
- O Lord, I know the way of man is not in himself;
  It is not in man who walks to direct his own steps (Jeremiah 10:23).
- The heart is deceitful above all things,
  And desperately wicked;
  Who can know it? (Jeremiah 17:9).

Since 1) God is infinite in wisdom and knowledge, and since 2) He created man, and since 3) He desires what is good for man, would it not stand to reason that He would understand the nature of man's problems, and that He would know the solution(s) to those problems? If you answer "Yes!", and you were sitting at the table described above, not a second thought would be given to whom you would ask your questions.

The point of this particular lesson is that God knows the solutions to our problems. This book centers on how to effectively cope with problems. So, the most effective way to cope is to be familiar with the biblical texts that relate to your issues of life. If we are not willing to acknowledge, or have not yet learned to acknowledge, that God knows the solutions to our problems, we are denying ourselves the help we need to cope with the issue we face. And because some lack faith in God to help them, for all practical intents and purposes, we have resorted to secular advice for spiritual problems, problems of living.

Take note of these passages:

- Trust in the Lord with all your heart,
  And lean not on your own understanding;
  In all your ways acknowledge Him,
  And He shall direct your paths.
  Do not be wise in your own eyes;
  Fear the Lord and depart from evil.
  It will be health to your flesh,
  And strength to your bones (Proverbs 3:5-8).

- All Scripture is given by inspiration of God, and is profitable for doctrine, for reproof, for correction, for instruction in righteousness, that the man of God may be complete, thoroughly equipped for every good work (2 Timothy 3:16-17).

- Grace and peace be multiplied to you in the knowledge of God and of Jesus our Lord, as His divine power has given to us all things that pertain to life and godliness, through the knowledge of Him who called us by glory and virtue (2 Peter 1:3).

- Peter exhorts us to cast all our anxiety upon God, "for He cares for you" (1 Peter 5:7).

The majority of our problems are summarily categorized by the apostle John as "the lust of the flesh, the lust of the eyes, and the pride of life" (1 John 2:16). These three are "all that is in the world." And "all that is in the world...is not of the Father but is of the world. And the world is passing away, and the lust of it; but he who does the will of God abides forever" (1 John 2:17).

One or more of these three things has overcome all of us. The question is, "How can we overcome them?" John answers: "For whatever is born of God overcomes the world. And this is the victory that has overcome the world—our faith" (1 John 5:4). And what is faith? It is trusting that what we have learned from God in His Word is true. It is a confidence that compels us to act on what we know!

I cannot over-emphasize how important this is. If an individual were fully persuaded that God's Word contained the solution to their problem, how much more diligent would they be in searching it for solutions? On the other hand, if an individual were not persuaded that God "bothers" Himself with our day-to-day problems, how diligent would they be in their search through the Scriptures?

Consider the relationship that exists between the first three chapters. We must acknowledge that:

- glorifying God is the primary purpose of my life

- we have all sinned and fallen short of the glory of God

- God knows the solutions to my problems

The Scriptures affirm that those who are right with God are those who live by faith—faith in God and in His Word (Hab. 2:4; Romans 1:17). Faith is trust, confidence. Our primary purpose in life is to glorify God. A life without faith does not glorify God and leads to sin; and sin is the problem.

How effective can the Scriptures be in addressing the 21st Century problems of man? Even though we may have advanced technologically, man himself has not changed. His nature is the same; temptations are the same; and the solutions are the same as they were 2,000 years ago.

A research psychiatrist, E. Fuller Torrey, argues that about 75 percent of the problems psychiatrists address are problems of living, 5 percent are organic brain disorders, and 20 percent "will require closer examination to make a final judgment." Martin and Deidre Bobgan, in their book *How to Counsel from Scripture*, concluded:

> Therefore, most people seeking help need the kind of counsel in which the Bible excels: how to live, how to relate to others, how to find meaning in life, how to know God, and how to become the kind of person God wants.

And,

> For Christians, problems that can be treated by psychological counseling can be better ministered to by biblical counsel within the body of Christ" (Bobgan 1985, p. 7).

Psychotherapy is the only form of treatment which, at least to some extent, appears to create the illness it treats. —Dr. Jerome D. Frank

Since the invasion of modern-day psychology, Christians have been intimidated into thinking that God's Word is no longer effective in dealing with the real issues men face. Do not be intimidated. The Bible is still the most relevant Book ever produced. It provides for us answers and solutions for our questions about life. Therein are found the principles for most effectively coping with our problems.

What we need to do is repent of our wrong attitudes and unbelief toward God and His Word, and once again recognize Him as the all-knowing and all-wise God that He is. Then we need to search His Word as though we were searching for hidden treasures, for gems of truth that will guide us effectively through this life.

THE GOD OF YOUR CHOICE?

To effectively cope with our problems, our faith must be in the true and living God and not in the god of our own choosing or invention.

What is disturbing about secular support groups that use the Twelve-Step approach is that some are really teaching people to have faith in faith. Let me explain. The third step in these Twelve Step Programs is: "I made a decision to turn my will and my life over to the care of God as we understand Him." Here, a formula is provided, but no content. They say you must trust God with your problem, but they do not identify who God is. "God" becomes whatever or whomever you make of Him - "as you understand Him." I am told by a friend of mine who is familiar with these programs that one gentleman identified his "higher power" as an article he clipped out of a newspaper and kept in his wallet.

Please do not misunderstand me. The true and living God is not excluded from all of these groups, but the exclusive proclamation of Him would not be welcome unless it was a Christian based group.

What people face when they go to a secular 12-Step program parallels what the apostle Paul faced when he was preaching the

Gospel in Athens. Among the myriads of idols that lined the streets of the academic center of the ancient world was an altar with this inscription, "TO AN UNKNOWN GOD" (Acts 17:23).

I fail to see how wholeness can be achieved in any counseling situation that is not based on a proper concept of God. This being the case, much of our work in handling problems will involve setting forth the true nature of God to those who may be "worshiping" Him in ignorance.

The reader might ask, "If an individual joins one of these support groups and trusts in a 'higher power' that does not correspond with reality, how do we account for their success?" Their higher power was actually in their power to believe. This is fideism, faith in faith.

The secular Twelve-Step programs do not guard against false ideas about God. You could be a pantheist or atheist and still enjoy a degree of success through these groups. The Twelve-Step programs, to appeal to the largest audience possible, are powerless to give a true picture of God. And they are powerless to deal with the issue of sin. In fact, some deny the reality of sin.

CONCLUDING REMARKS

The only way someone can overcome the real problem of sin is to place his or her confidence in God and His Word. All else falls short of complete recovery.

What does all of this have to do with our lesson? Precisely this: the object of our faith is crucial. If the object of our faith is not God, the Creator of heaven and earth, we are simply healing our hurt a little.

FAITH WORKSHEET

It is amazing how many people hinder God by believing that He deals only with those things that relate to their initial salvation and "spiritual" matters, but that He is not concerned with the practical issues of life. Friend, many of our problems are spiritual problems. And yet we either do not believe or do not know that God's Word addresses even the practical matters of life (i.e., friendships, marriage, family matters, finances, addiction, unbelief, communication problems, etc.).

Solomon asked the question, "For who knows what is good for man in life, all the days of his vain life which he passes like a shadow? Who can tell a man what will happen after him under the sun?" (Ecclesiastes 6:12).

God is infinite in His wisdom and knowledge. He created man and desires what is best for him. Does it not stand to reason that He knows and understands what man's problems are and that He knows, and would make known the solutions to those who wanted to know?

The issue here is really one of faith. The degree of confidence you have in God's Word will dictate the degree or intensity with which you search His Word for answers and solutions. The late Gus Nichols, a wise mature preacher, used to ask three questions of anyone who came to him for counsel.

- Are you willing to do what is right?

- Are you willing to do what is right, right now?

- Are you willing to let the Bible determine what is right?

Think About It

1. In what direction do some people turn seeking solutions to their problems? (i.e., drugs, alcohol, sex, music, secular counseling).

2. In what direction have you turned seeking solutions to your problem(s)?

3. In what way has the direction you have turned helped you? hindered you? not provided you with the direction you needed?

4. What efforts have you made to seek God's solution to the issues with which you struggle?

5. What is it that has hindered you from seeking the wise counsel that comes from God through His Word?

6. Richard Ganz asks: "What has brought us to the place where we Christians feel we cannot deal with our problems without the help of popular psychology?" (Psycho Babble, Wheaton, Illinois, Crossway Books, 1993, p. 61).

Examples from the Scriptures

1. Read Isaiah 30:1-5

   a. How had Israel added sin to sin?

   b. What would result from Israel turning to Egypt for their help?

   c. How did Israel's turning to Egypt for help manifest their lack of faith?

2. Read Jeremiah 2:9-13

a. What were the two evils God's people had committed?

b. What evidence is there that Christians today exchange their God for those who are no gods?

4

SOLUTION

One's view of the Scriptures is dependent on one's view of God.
—Kevin Vanhooser

The two premises on which this book is written are 1) that the Bible is the Word of God (2 Timothy 3:16; 2 Peter 1:20-21) and 2) it contains "all things that pertain to life and godliness, through the knowledge of Him who called us to glory and virtue" (2 Peter 1:3).

It grieves me no little bit to hear some professed believers argue that the Bible did not offer them the help they needed to cope with a problem of living. It has been my experience that those who claim the Bible is insufficient either did not search the Scriptures for their answers or they did not search them enough.

One brother told me he could not find help in the Scriptures for his problem, but that he found help through a secular support

47

group. I asked him to look back at what he had learned, to reflect on his knowledge of the Word, and to tell me what he had learned in the support group that, upon further reflection, he could not have concluded having read the Scriptures. After some reflection, he admitted that there was nothing he learned that he could not have found in the Bible if he had only thought it through. He has become a grateful advocate for the sufficiency of God's Word. The primary thing the support group supplied for him was commiseration for his experience as a child of drunkard.

Another reason some do not believe the Bible is informationally sufficient is that some people simply do not desire the counsel that Scripture gives.

The primary point of Lesson Three is that God, our Creator, being infinite in His knowledge and wisdom, knows the solutions to our problems. The main point of this lesson is that those solutions can be found in His Word, the Bible.

THE SCRIPTURES
Let's see what God affirms about His Word.

Paul wrote to Timothy:

All Scripture is given by inspiration of God, and is profitable for doctrine, for reproof, for correction, for instruction, that the man of God may be complete, thoroughly equipped for every good work" (2 Timothy 3:16,17).

First of all, Paul affirms that the Scriptures are profitable. They are profitable because they are inspired, which means they are "God-breathed" or the very product of God. Peter wrote, "for prophecy never came by the will of man, but holy men of God spoke as they were moved by the Holy Spirit" (2 Peter 1:21). It is not the product of any man's own scheme or ideas (see 2 Peter 1:21). Its penmen did not follow cunningly devised fables.

The Scriptures are profitable because they are able to save. James wrote, "Therefore lay aside all filthiness and overflow of wickedness, and receive with meekness the implanted word, which is able to save your souls" (James 1:21). The Bible is profitable because it contains words whereby we may be saved from sin. Sometimes we may think that the Bible deals with subject matter that does not appear relevant to us. This is not a problem inherent with the Bible. We simply lack the wisdom and understanding to see how the Bible relates to us. For example, if we are not convinced that sin is at the root of our problems, then the Bible will appear irrelevant, but that is not because it is. It is because have not yet seen the connection between sin and our problems.

An *holusion* illustrates the point. A holusion is a computer-created picture that, at first, looks like random marks on a page, but once you learn how to focus your eyes just right you see a picture emerge. Once your vision is clearly focused on the picture, it creates the illusion of a three-dimensional image of remarkable clarity. I have watched others try to find the picture in one of these holusions; some see the picture within a few minutes, others take a few hours. (It took me half a day to see my first picture.)

The Scriptures can be like these holusions. At first they may not seem relevant. Their teachings may seem unrelated to our problems and circumstances. That is not because they are unrelated, but rather it is because we have not yet learned to focus our "eyes" to see how they address our problems.

The Scriptures are also profitable because they will abide forever. Solutions preached by secular counselors change on a fairly regular basis, but the truth of God's Word stands forever. That's why Solomon could say, "buy the truth and sell it not" (Proverbs 23:23). It does not change. Some of the "solutions" prescribed by men are bought and sold on a regular basis. With God's Word, we do not need to wait for updates or for some better prescription for our problems.

The Scriptures, being the Word of God, are inerrant - that is, they cannot be wrong about anything. They are inerrant because God knows everything that is subject to being known and it is impossible for Him to lie (Titus 1:2; Hebrews 6:18). Because they are authoritative, man is warned against adding to them or taking away from them or twisting them beyond their intended meaning. (See 2 Peter 3:16; Revelation 22:18-19; Galatians 1:6-11.)

Having examined some of the reasons why the Scriptures are profitable, let's now see how they are profitable. First of all, Paul tells us that they are profitable for "teaching" ("doctrine," some translations). These teachings are profitable because they are from God. Contained within the pages of the Bible is the whole counsel of God. They contain all things that pertain to life and godliness through the knowledge of God (2 Peter 1:3).

They are profitable for reproof. Reproof is closely connected to doctrine or teaching. When we live in a way that conflicts with God's will, we subject ourselves to His reproof. Not only do the Scriptures provide us with teachings on how to live, they provide us with reproofs for letting us know when we are walking contrary to their principles and laws. The Bible is a spiritual check-and-balance system.

> Only psychology, we are told, can divine our secret motivations and reveal the elusive 'why' of the strange human animal. The rules of discovery require professional interpretation. Just as the clergy once mediated between man and his soul, so the psychiatric and psychological profession must now interpret the mind for man. — Martin Gross

The Bible is also profitable for correction. This is perhaps the most pertinent point, as it relates to the basic purpose of this book. When our lives are in turmoil and we want to straighten them out to live productive God-honoring lives, the Scriptures provide us with responsible steps of action for returning to sound/healthy living.

For example, if "homosexuality" is the problem, and the counselor approves of homosexuality, what course of action or guidance do you think the "patient" would receive? Will the secular humanist or atheistic counselor provide responsible steps of action for those whom they counsel? Would they be counseled to cease such behavior, or would the counselor simply try to sear the "patient's" conscience concerning homosexuality? The Bible is profitable because it provides responsible steps of action to correct the error in peoples' lives.

Some receive no correction at all from those whom they seek counsel. A session might go something like this:

Counselor: Why are you here?

Counselee: I have a problem. I am involved in homosexuality.

(One psychologist admitted he has never had someone tell him that they have a problem with heterosexuality.)

Counselor: What is the problem?

Counselee: I want to know what I can do to help myself.

Counselor: What do you think you should do?

The counselee is asked what he thinks he should do. He is never given instructions on what he ought to do. What else can they do? They have no objective standard to appeal to in a counseling situation. They have nothing but a smorgasbord of psychological theories from which to choose.

The Scriptures are profitable for instruction. Instruction brings us back, full circle, to the teaching of Scripture reinforcing what had been taught and perhaps forgotten or neglected.

Paul wrote that through the Scriptures the man of God may be complete, furnished completely unto every good work. A man cannot be complete without God and His Word. A man without God is a man in conflict. A man without God's Word is not sufficiently equipped to cope with his problems.

To find God's solutions may require a great deal of effort, but the benefits are worth the effort. When faced with any issue of life we need to ask ourselves: "How does God address my problem in His Word?" and then we need to search His Word for the answers.

This all ties in with the previous chapter in an important way. God's word is profitable to its full extent when someone believes it. Paul commended the Thessalonians, writing,

> For this reason we also thank God without ceasing, because when you received the word of God which you heard from us, you welcomed it not as the word of men, but as it is in truth, the word of God, which also effectively works in you who believe (1 Thessalonians 2:13).

The Word of God works in those who believe.

The writer of Hebrews exhorts his readers: "For indeed the gospel was preached to us as well as to them; but the word which they heard did not profit them, not being mixed with faith in those who heard it" (Hebrews 4:2). Paul said the Scriptures are profitable for doctrine, for reproof, for correction, for instruction in righteousness. But if they are not united by faith with them that hear, they are neither profitable for doctrine, or reproof or correction or instruction. Unless what we hear is united with faith, it will profit us nothing.

QUESTION: Why did God find it necessary to provide and preserve for us His Word in written form? Could not man, upon enough reflection, reason out for himself the contents found therein? The Scriptures are essential, as can be understood by the fact that it is not in man that walks to direct his own steps (Jeremiah 10:23). Man needs teaching, reproof, correction, and instruction from God to know how to live well.

Grappling with some problems may require life long effort. Some solutions are simpler than others and require nothing more than discovering the error and supplanting it with the truth. For other problems there are no quick solutions—but there are solutions. To live life in a way that honors God, we need to be willing to pay whatever the price might be to overcome them. It may require a life-long effort on our part, but, oh, the blessedness that will be ours when we do.

WISDOM

Solomon, the wise king of old, said that silver and gold are not worthy to be compared with the value of truth and wisdom from God. Of wisdom he said:

- …seek her as silver, and search for her as for hidden treasures (Proverbs 2:4).

- She is more precious than rubies. And all the things you may desire cannot compare with her (Proverbs 3:15).

- My fruit is better than gold, yes, than fine gold, And my revenue than choice silver (Proverbs 8:19).

- How much better it is to get wisdom than gold! And to understand is to be chosen rather than silver (Proverbs 16:16).

SOLUTIONS WORKSHEET

Charles Colson visited a prison near Oslo Norway.

I was greeted by the warden, a psychiatrist with a clinically detached attitude. As she showed me through the sterile surroundings, which seemed more like a laboratory than a prison, she touted the number of counselors and the types of therapies given to inmates. In fact, we met so many other psychiatrists that I asked the warden how many of the inmates were mental cases.

"All of them, of course," she replied quickly, raising her eyebrows in surprise.

"What do you mean, 'all of them'?"

"Well, anyone who commits a violent crime is obviously mentally unbalanced."

Ah, yes. People are basically good, so anyone who could do something so terrible must be mentally ill. And the solution is therapy. I was seeing the therapeutic model fully realized.

Some tells us that in order for a person to understand the nature of their problem that lengthy and intense treatment by a psychiatrist or psychological professional is required. "Only psychology," we are told, "can divine our secret motives and reveal the elusive 'why' of the strange human animal" (Gross 1978, p. 14).

Compare this notion with Hebrews 4:12-13:

> For the word of God is living, and active, and sharper than any two-edged sword, and piercing even to the dividing of soul and spirit, of both joints and marrow, and quick to discern the thoughts and intents of the heart. And there is no creature that is not manifest in his sight: but all things are naked and laid open before the eyes of him with whom we have to do.

The Scriptures reveal the truth about the history it tells, and they reveal the hidden motives and attitudes of the characters it presents. The characters they sketch may make us uncomfortable because we so closely resemble them.

> The characters in the Gospel accounts "...are sketched with sure strokes, but not so fully as to preclude our identifying ourselves with them. Their faces are never so completely drawn that we cannot place our own heads on their shoulders: we could be blind, man, neighbor, parent, or Pharisee, and it can be instructive for us to assume each role in turn as we read" —Roland Frye

What do the Scriptures claim for themselves?

1. Psalm 12:6

2. Romans 1:16

3. 1 Corinthians 2:10-13

4. Galatians 1:11-12

5. 2 Timothy 3:16-17

6. 2 Peter 1:3

7. 2 Peter 1:20-21

8. Revelation 19:9

Consider the following passages as they relate the Scriptures to the issues of life:

1. Romans 15:4

2. 1 Corinthians 10:11

3. Hebrews 11:1ff

4. James 1:23-24

THINK ABOUT IT

Christians are a people of the Book. But can we be a people of the Book if the credibility, reliability, and relevance of that Book are in question?

Although theology is taken from two words that, together, mean "the study of God," many brothers and sisters prefer shortcuts to "relevance." To say that theology is boring is really to say that God is boring. And yet, part of the problem is that the average person in the pew is not likely to get a steady diet of theology that is proclaimed with excitement and relevance. How can we think about God's character and actions in history and yawn? Who would dare say that the God of the Bible is irrelevant for the modern world? The Creator of heaven and earth, the One who has all of history in His hand, the Lord of history, is relevant to everything we do. —R. C. Sproul

1. Why are the credibility, reliability, and relevance of the Scriptures brought into question today?

2. Why is it important for us to have complete confidence in the Bible as the Word of God and for us to recognize it as our primary textbook for all of life?

EXAMPLES FROM THE SCRIPTURES

1. Read Matt. 4:1-11

    a. How did Jesus confront Satan in each phase of His temptation?

    b. What connection is there between the temptation we face and the Scriptures?

2. Read 2 Kings 22-23

    a. How did the finding of the Book of the Law affect Josiah?

    b. What resulted?

READ AND MEDITATE

1. Psalm 119 - list all of the characteristics of the Word of God that you can find, along with the benefits that can be derived from it.

STEVEN M. LLOYD

5

SUCCESS

I have treasured up the words of his mouth more than my necessary food.
—Job

Most of us deal with problems only when our lives become unmanageable. Only then will we address them. And once we find a solution, we work it until the pain of the problem begins to subside. But once life becomes marginally manageable we slack off working through the issue to its resolution, and the monster we thought we had control over once again rears its ugly head.

Why do we wait for a problem to become unavoidable or unmanageable before we ever begin to address it?

THE KEY TO SUCCESS

Lasting results come to those who meditate on God's Word continually. When one ceases to meditate on God's Word success in effectively coping with problems will diminish. The only way to ensure lasting results is to ponder, or to think on God's Word day and night.

Moses' successor, Joshua, was given the formidable task of taking possession of the Promised Land. Needless to say, there were many challenges to face. (Read the Book of Joshua.) When Joshua was commissioned by God to lead Israel into the land of promise, he was told:

> This Book of the Law shall not depart from your mouth, but you shall meditate in it day and night, that you may observe to do according to all that is written in it. For then you will make your way prosperous, and then you will have good success (Joshua 1:8).

Notice how often meditation is related to prosperity and good success. The mark of a good leader is that he is a good follower of God. And the only way to be an effective follower is to meditate on God's Word.

The blessed man of Psalm One not only avoids the counsel of the wicked, the way of sinners and the seat of scoffers,

> But his delight is in the law of the Lord,
> And in His law he meditates day and night (Psalm 1:2).

After comparing him to a fruitful, prosperous, healthy tree, we are told, "And whatever he does shall prosper" (Psalm 1:3).

Consider some of the benefits of meditating on God's Word as enumerated in Psalm 119:97-104:

- you will be wiser than your enemies
- you will have more understanding than all your teachers

- you will have more understanding than the aged
- you will refrain your feet from every evil way
- you will get understanding
- you will hate every false way.

Most of the counseling I have ever been a part of centered around helping a person change the way they think. It involved correcting some wrong or false notion about God or correcting someone's thinking about the very nature of man. Consequently, most counseling sessions become Bible studies. Having listened to the case, and having asked whatever questions I felt were necessary to get at the heart of a problem, I then direct our attention to the light of Scripture.

I am sad to say that after one session, a woman said rather disappointedly, "Well, that's what I thought you'd say." When I asked her what she meant, she told me, "I knew you would just give me Bible passages to consider." Pray tell, what else or what better could I give her?!

ENSURING LASTING RESULTS

The focus of this lesson is on ensuring lasting results where our conflicts in life are concerned. The key to lasting results is meditating continually on God's Word. As one meditates on the Word, so goes his or her success. When we cease to reflect on God's Word, we unfortunately fail to keep ourselves plugged in to our power source, and failure is inevitable. When we remove God and His solutions from our thinking, we are doomed to repeated failure.

Consider the implications of the following two passages. Paul wrote to the church in Philippi:

> Therefore, my beloved, as you have always obeyed, not as in my presence only, but now much more in my absence, work out your own salvation with fear and trembling; for it is God who works in you both to will and to do for His good pleasure (Philippians 2:12-13).

To the church of the Thessalonians:

> For this reason we also thank God without ceasing, because when you received the word of God which you heard from us, you welcomed it not as the word of men, but as it is in truth, the word of God, which also effectively works in you who believe (1 Thessalonians 2:13).

The passage in Philippians makes it clear that it is God who works in the believer "to will and to do" for God's good pleasure. Two of the ingredients that cause apathy and slothfulness toward doing the will of God are a lack of desire and a lack of energy. "To will" addresses the issue of desire and "to do" addresses the energy shortage. (The Greek word, here translated "to do," is the word from which we get our word "energy.") The point is this: if we lack the desire or the energy to do what honors God it follows that we are not letting God work in us.

But how is it that God works in us? In the Thessalonian passage, Paul praises his brethren because when he preached to them they received the word of the message as "the word of God" and not as the word of men. They received his message, "as it is in truth, the word of God, which also effectively works in you who believe." So, it is God's word that effectively works in us and motivates us to do His will.

The writer of Hebrews characterizes God's Word as:

> ...living, and powerful, and sharper than any two-edged sword, piercing

even to the division of soul and spirit, and of joints and marrow, and is a discerner of the thoughts and intents of the heart. And there is no creature hidden from His sight, but all things are naked and open to the eyes of Him to whom we must give account" (Hebrews 4:12,13).

God's Word is so powerful that when it takes up residence in the heart, God works in those who believe. He provides them with the motivation and the energy they need to sustain them for His good pleasure.

God's Word does more than sustain us. It transforms us. It ultimately alters our behavior. For example, one author relates the story of a man struggling with the issue of homosexuality. The troubled man promised the counselor that he would never practice it again. The counselor told him not to promise never to commit the act again, but rather to promise that he would begin meditating on Scripture. After committing to memory numerous passages on the subject the struggling man's desires changed, which resulted in a change in his behavior.

A change in our behavior is brought about by a change in the way we think. A change in the way we think is brought about through meditating on God's living-active-sharper-than-any-two-edged-sword Word. Paul affirms this in his exhortation to the brethren in Rome:

> I beseech you therefore, brethren, by the mercies of God, that you present your bodies a living sacrifice, holy, acceptable to God, which is your reasonable service. And do not be conformed to this world, but be transformed by the renewing of your mind, that you may prove what is that good and acceptable and perfect will of God (Romans 12:1-2).

By meditating on God's Word, we are no longer being conformed to the world but we are being transformed by the renewing of our mind. And in so doing we prove God's will to be good and acceptable and perfect (complete).

The transformation takes place "by the renewing of your mind." This means you will no longer think as you once did. The way you thought prior to the transformation is most likely the cause of your problem(s). But when the mind is renewed in terms of quality, it will be fresh, unworn thinking. Just imagine how this could be the case for you!

Something else to consider is that you do not affect the transformation by yourself. Paul wrote of "being transformed." It is God working in you through the agency of His powerful, life-altering, transforming Word. R. C. Trench described the renewing process as,

> …the gradual conforming of the man more and more to that new spiritual world into which he has been introduced, and in which he now lives and moves; the restoration of the divine image; and in all this, so far from being passive, he must be a fellow-worker with God. (McGuiggan 1982, p. 349).

Jesus said, "Man shall not live by bread alone, but by every word that proceeds from the mouth of God" (Matthew 4:4). We rarely miss a meal as the day goes by and yet we will go for long periods of time without feeding our souls the Word of God— periods of time that would kill us if we did not eat the food needful to the body. HOW CAN WE HOPE TO SURVIVE UNDER SUCH CONDITIONS?! (Pardon me for raising my voice.)

We need to have the attitude of Job: "I have treasured up the words of his mouth more than my necessary food" (Job 23:12).

THE PURPOSE OF MEDITATION

The purpose of meditation is two-fold. First of all, it helps us to bring into captivity every thought to the obedience of Christ (2 Corinthians 10:5). In so doing we learn what thoughts of ours are in error. Once identified, we can replace erroneous ideas with the truth. Not only do we learn wherein we err in our thinking, we also ensure ourselves against a relapse into faulty thinking by continually meditating on the Word.

Secondly, meditating on God's Word is preventive in nature. Imagine the difference between facing a problem while ignorant of God's will on the subject and facing a problem armed with the truth and divine solution to the problem. A lack of knowledge can destroy us just like it did Israel of old (Hosea 4:6). Wisdom is looking at life from God's perspective. Our problems usually stem from not being able to see or being unwilling to look at life in this way. Imagine being able to look at the various circumstances of life from His perspective! Oh, what a difference it would make.

SOWING AND REAPING

There are certain principles of agriculture that may help us to see the value of meditation. The most rudimentary of all is the principle of sowing, which is simply this: you must sow something before you can reap something. The question, as it applies to our point is this: what are you sowing or planting in your mind?

A second principle is that you reap what you sow. If a man sows corn in the earth, he will reap corn. "He that sows iniquity shall reap calamity" (Proverbs 22:8). If a man is sowing the Word of God in his mind he will reap the rich benefits promised in it.

Of course, there are numerous other applications that could be drawn from the principles of harvesting, but these will suffice for the purpose at hand.

So, how can we ensure lasting results in coping with problems? By meditating on God's Word continually and by whole-hearted submission to it.

SUCCESS WORKSHEET

According to the passages that follow, what is the key to all successful living?

1. Joshua 1:8

2. Psalm 1:1-3

3. Psalm 119:97-104

4. Isaiah 26:3

5. Philippians 4:8

6. 1 Timothy 4:15

Now look back at each one of these passages and list some of the benefits that are derived from meditating on God's Word.

To ensure lasting results when facing the issues of life we must meditate continually on the Word of God. Meditating on His Word will change the way we think; and a change in the way we think will produce a change in the way we behave. The Psalmist draws this same connection for us when he writes:

Your word have I hidden in my heart,

That I might not sin against You" (Psalm 119:11)

Other passages affirm that the wonderful transformation that takes place occurs by means of a renewing of our mind. Note carefully how this truth is expressed in the following passages:

1. Romans 12:1-2 2.

2. 2 Corinthians 4:16-18

3. Ephesians 4:17-24

4. Colossians 3:1-2, 10

The purpose of being transformed by the renewing of our mind to prove that God's will is good and acceptable (pleasing) and perfect.

THINK ABOUT IT

1. If meditating on the Scriptures is so critical to the health and well-being of the soul, what should we expect when such is not practiced?

2. What is the connection between Philippians 2:12-13 and 1 Thessalonians 2:13?

3. In order to change our behavior, what must occur?

Meditation is nothing more than thinking long about something. The object of thought, in the meditation encouraged in the Bible, is the Word of God. And our thinking on the ideas and truths of Scripture is to be continuous—day and night.

In order for us to consider the Scriptures all day long, we must familiarize ourselves with them enough to store them up in our hearts. Whatever this requires of us is worth the price. Here I would also recommend that you work with paragraphs of Scripture - not just a verse here and a verse there. Keep a note pad handy to jot down questions that may arise, and to record the things you learn. This will help you engage in an active reading of Scripture.

I dare say that the degree of success we enjoy in doing this will determine whether we make it out of this life sane or otherwise.

A word to the wise: Samuel Thompson, in his book *A Modern Philosophy of Religion*, argues:

> I could be guilty of no greater presumption than to make my knowledge and what I happen to understand the measure of reason itself; it would be to assume that I myself am the source of reason and of the intelligibility which belongs to things. 'The worst snob in the world,' Sydney Harris points out, 'is the uncultivated man who smugly believes that whatever he does not understand is meaningless, or else he could understand it" (Thompson 1956, p. 5).

Please do not underestimate the effectiveness of what has been presented in this chapter if you have not tested it for yourself. In fact, I would venture to say that a failure to practice the things mentioned in this chapter is the very reason most people never learn to cope as effectively as they could with the issue of their life.

READ AND MEDITATE

1. Psalm 1
2. Psalm 119:97-104

6

ATTITUDE

The Christians are right; it is Pride that has been the chief cause of misery in every nation and every family since the world began. Other vices may sometimes bring people together; you may find good fellowship and jokes and friendliness among drunken people or unchaste people. But Pride always means enmity—it is enmity. And not only enmity between man and man, but enmity to God. —C. S. Lewis

It is said that pride is the only disease that makes everyone sick but the one who has it. Pride erects one of the greatest barriers against coping effectively with life. The wise King Solomon said:

- When pride comes, then comes shame;
  But with the humble is wisdom (Proverbs 11:2).

- By pride comes only contention,
  But with the well-advised is wisdom (Proverbs 13:10).

- Pride goes before destruction,
  And a haughty spirit before a fall (Proverbs 16:18).

- A man's pride will bring him low,

69

But the humble in spirit will retain honor (Proverbs 29:23).

The opposite of pride is humility. Humility is present when one thinks no more highly of himself than he ought to think (Romans 12:3). Humility is the honest acknowledgment of our true condition.

Humility is recognizable, and it can lead to great joy. For example, King David recognized this quality of humility in his life when he wrote:

Lord, my heart is not haughty,
> Nor my eyes lofty.
> Neither do I concern myself with great matters,
> Nor with things too profound for me.
Surely I have calmed and quieted my soul,
> Like a weaned child with his mother;
> Like a weaned child is my soul within me.
O Israel, hope in the Lord
From this time forth and forever (Psalm 131).

But acknowledging the presence of a humble spirit gives us nothing to boast of. It is the very fact that we have nothing to boast of that humbles us.

To effectively cope with conflict, we must humble ourselves. Grace is given to the humble. The proud are resisted (James 4:6ff).

POOR IN SPIRIT

Jesus' opening words in the Sermon on the Mount are "Blessed are the poor in spirit; for theirs is the kingdom of heaven" (Matt. 5:3). There were two Greek words at His disposal to convey the idea of poverty. One word points to the man who must work for a living because he owns no property and must live frugally (Gk., *penes*). The other word refers to complete destitution, a condition that forces the poor to seek help from others by begging (Gk., *ptochos*). This second word represents a much greater degree of poverty. It is also the word Jesus used in the first beatitude.

Hugo McCord makes this observation with reference to the level of poverty symbolized by the word *ptochos*:

> The man Jesus described is not in tolerably bad circumstances. He is a beggar . . . A beggar is desperate . . . If there is no mercy he knows he must die (McCord 1956, p. 12).

The word under discussion is used to describe Lazarus as opposed to the rich man (Luke 16:20-21). Lazarus was thrown down at the rich man's gate, left only with the desire to be fed the crumbs that fell from the rich man's table while the dogs licked the sores that covered his body (16:19).

The word is also used by James concerning the man who came to worship God dressed in vile clothing. His level of poverty is contrasted with the rich man who wore the fine clothing. Both men are used to teach against showing favor to one man above another (James 2:1-13).

When Jesus spoke of the blessed being "poor in spirit," He was referring to those who are humble. To be poor in spirit is to be empty. It is only when a person realizes what their true condition is that they will be in the right frame of mind to accept help from God. Otherwise, they will think of themselves as self-sufficient; self-confident; self-reliant; self-righteous.

The apostle Paul received visions and revelations from the

Lord. But lest he become too arrogant there was given to him a "thorn in the flesh, a messenger of Satan" to keep him in line "lest I should be exalted above measure." He prayed three times for God to remove this malady, but God responded by saying, "My grace is sufficient for you: for My strength is made perfect in weakness." Paul's response to all of this was: "Therefore most gladly I will rather boast in my infirmities, that the power of Christ may rest upon me" (See 2 Corinthians 12:1-10).

The point Paul is making is this: it is only when we are willing to acknowledge our weak and frail condition that we will open the door for God to work in our lives. If we come to view ourselves as "strong" and "self-sufficient" we will not acknowledge our desperate need for God.

Humility requires that we think no more highly of ourselves than we ought to think (Romans 12:3). It is acknowledging before God and others our true condition. Only then will God give grace to us (1 Peter 5:5).

Many people live their lives burdened with problems they are not able to bear alone. Because of their proud heart, they will not admit that they need help nor will they seek help. Consequently, their burden is intensified. With pride comes shame, and contention, and destruction. With poverty of spirit comes wisdom and honor.

Pride, then, becomes a primary factor in our failures to cope effectively.

King David had transgressed the will of God when he committed adultery with Bathsheba. Rather than confess his fault before God, in pride he kept silent for a time.

> When I kept silent, my bones grew old
> Through my groaning all the day long.
> For day and night Your hand was heavy upon me;
> My vitality was turned into the drought of summer (Psalm 32:3-4).

It was only when he humbled himself before God that he experienced relief:

> I acknowledged my sin to You,
> And my iniquity I have not hidden.
> I said, "I will confess my transgressions to the Lord,"
> And You forgave the iniquity of my sin (32:5).

We do nothing but compound our problems when we are unwilling to acknowledge our weak and frail condition before God. When we are "strong" we do not let God work, but when we are "weak" then God is strong; His strength is made perfect (complete).

You may be saying to yourself, "But my problem isn't a sin problem." I would encourage you to ask yourself a few questions:

- Are you sure it isn't a sin problem (yours or someone else's)?

- How open are you to receive help from others?

The reason you may be having difficulty coping with some issue(s) is that you are too proud to admit you have a problem or too proud to seek help.

The writers of Scripture affirm that God resists the proud but gives grace to the humble (James 4:6; 1 Peter 5:5; both are quoting Proverbs 3:34). Because He resists the proud, James writes:

> Therefore submit to God. Resist the devil and he will flee from you.
> Draw near to God and He will draw near to you. Cleanse your hands,
> you sinners; and purify your hearts, you double-minded. Lament and
> mourn and weep! Let your laughter be turned to mourning and your joy
> to gloom. Humble yourselves in the sight of the Lord, and He will lift
> you up (James 4:7-10).

Peter writes,

> Therefore humble yourselves under the mighty hand of God, that He
> may exalt you in due time, casting all your care upon Him, for He cares
> for you (1 Peter 5:6-7).

Since God does not favor pride, pride would obviously be the
wrong way to respond to a problem. Since God gives grace (His
favor) to the humble (that is, the poor in spirit), we should
approach our problems with humility toward God.

How does one become poor in spirit? Poverty in spirit refers
to being empty. It is only when people recognize their own
inadequacy and unprofitableness that they are in the right frame of
mind to accept the help that comes from God.

This was, perhaps, one of the most difficult points for me to
grasp as a young Christian. I had trouble believing that I was as
bad off as the Scriptures made me out to be. When I compared
myself with others my age I looked pretty good. I didn't drink,
cuss (much), smoke, carouse with girls, or do drugs. We can all
find someone that makes us look good, but when our eyes are
opened and we begin measuring ourselves with the incomparable
Christ, then we are better able to see ourselves as God sees us.

I thought Romans 3:10 should be read: "There is none

righteous, no, not one, except Steve Lloyd...and others like him" —that is, until I learned what standard I ought to be comparing myself. Then I realized the "except Steve Lloyd" ought to be left off.

I can just hear someone saying, "But this kind of thinking will damage my self-esteem!" Don't worry about your self-esteem! Just learn to see yourself as God sees you and humbly accept the help He offers to fashion you more in the image of His Son, Jesus Christ. Learn to say with the apostle Paul, "And such confidence have we through Christ to God-ward: not that we are sufficient of ourselves, to account anything as from ourselves; but our sufficiency is from God" (2 Corinthians 3:4-5).

CAUTION: Seeing oneself in the light of Scripture has mistakenly led some to such extremes as masochism. People deprive their bodies of necessities of life and inflict themselves with beatings, as punishment for their sinful condition. This is an extreme that God does not require of those who would follow Him.

I might add that meditating on the Scriptures daily will go a long way toward helping you see your true condition. They will also provide you with responsible steps of action to remedy the situation in which you find yourself.

ATTITUDE WORKSHEET

When Jesus said, "Blessed are the poor in spirit," (Matthew 5:3) He used a word for poor that is equivalent to our word destitute.

> The man Jesus described is not in tolerably bad circumstances. He is a beggar…A beggar is desperate…If there is no mercy he knows he must die. —Hugo McCord

Notice how the word "poor" is used and with reference to whom:

1. Luke 16:20-21

2. James 2:2-3

3. 2 Corinthians 8:9

Notice the concept of poverty in spirit as it is expressed in the following:

1. Psalm 51:17

2. Isaiah 57:15

3. Romans 12:3

4. 2 Corinthians 3:5ff

5. Philippians 3:1-16

6. James 4:6

Now consider the contrasting attitude as expressed in the following:

1. 2 Corinthians 10:12

2. Luke 14:7-11

3. Luke 18:9-14

4. Revelation 3:14-22

THINK ABOUT IT

1. Why is humility such a critical quality in the management of the issues we face?

2. What obstacles are in the way of being poor in spirit?

3. How is one made humble?

4. Can a person be proud of their humility? (See Psalm 131)

EXAMPLES FROM THE SCRIPTURES

1. READ Daniel 4:28-37

   a. What fatal character flaw caused the downfall of the King?

   b. When was he restored to his right mind?

2. READ Obadiah 1-4, What was the fatal flaw that caused the destruction of Edom?

3. READ Luke 18:9-14

   a. To whom does Jesus address this parable?

   b. Which character in the parable is identified with those who trusted in themselves?

   c. How did he demonstrate his relationship with the self-righteous?

d. What lesson does Jesus want us to learn from this parable?

READ AND MEDITATE

1. Psalm 32

2. Psalm 51

3. 2 Corinthians 12:1-10

7

ACCOUNTABILITY

For we must all appear before the judgment seat of Christ, that each one may
receive the things done in the body, according to what he has done, whether
good or bad. —Paul

In 1982 I was invited to preach in Central California where a
good friend of mine labored. One of the topics I spoke on was
homosexuality. When services had concluded, and all of the
people filed out of the building, I noticed a woman standing off to
the side. I rightly assumed that she wanted to talk with me. When
she was able to speak to me in private she scolded me for being
ugly and insensitive toward "homosexuals."

After she exhausted herself at my expense I asked her if she
had time to visit. She said yes. We sat down. I reviewed my
lesson with her. In essence, I surveyed what the Bible had to say
on the subject, emphasizing that it does not really matter what
others or I may think. What matters is what God thinks. I

suggested that we love all people, but that we were to love all people without condoning sinful behavior. I also suggested that we should speak the truth on the subject with the hope that we might snatch some out of the fire (Jude 23).

Once my distraught critic had calmed down, the real reason for her hostility came out. She was not a member of the church, but her husband was. He had sexually molested both of their daughters, and both girls, at the time, were practicing lesbianism. She said, "My husband's actions toward them made them lesbians!" She blamed her husband for the lesbianism her daughters practiced. (I thought it was interesting that even though she was upset with me, she did not approve of her daughters' lifestyle anymore than God did and forbid them to practice such while staying in her home.)

Her husband was to blame for incest, but not for turning her daughters into lesbians. Not all women who have been sexually abused by their fathers become lesbians. It is a choice they make, perhaps influenced by their hatred for men due to what their father (or some other male) has done. There are other reasons people give for engaging in homosexuality than sexual abuse.

The important point here is to identify the right cause for the effect. As long as we place the blame for our own behavior on someone else, we will never learn to cope effectively with problems in life. The reason for this is that we will always view the source or the cause of the problem we face as resting with someone else. Consequently, we will place the responsibility for our actions on someone else. And as long as we are convinced that the responsibility lies with someone else we will never seek out effective responsible steps of action to correct our behavior.

THE BLAME GAME

When God confronted Adam with his disobedience in the Garden, the first man said, "The woman whom You gave to be with me, she gave me of the tree, and I ate" (Gen. 3:12). Adam even implicated God in his own defense. And when God confronted Eve, she tried to excuse herself by saying, "The serpent deceived me, and I ate" (3:13).

The "blame game" is one most of us have learned to play, and have learned to play very well. We have learned to play it so effectively that we have hurt ourselves when it comes to coping with our problems.

We must learn to acknowledge that we are accountable to God and to others for our actions. We are accountable to God because it is His will that we keep or break.

WHY SHOULD GOD BE SERVED?

Someone may ask, "But why should God be served?" or "Why am I accountable to Him?" Wayne Jackson, preacher for the East Main Church of Christ in Stockton, suggests six reasons in his sermon by the same title:

- because of who He is, because of His very nature

- because God is love (1 John 4:8; Romans. 5:8)

- because He is the Creator and we are His creatures

- because of the condition we are in (Romans. 3:23)

- for the sheer pleasure of it (Psalm 16:8)

- because not all accounts are settled in this life

Our life is given to us on loan, thus making us stewards of the life we possess. This is especially true for Christians:

> Or do you not know that your body is the temple of the Holy Spirit who is in you, whom you have from God, and you are not your own? For you were bought at a price; therefore glorify God in your body and in your spirit, which are God's (1 Corinthians 6:19-20).

Wendell Winkler, director of the Bible department at Faulkner University, brought this idea of stewardship into focus for me when he suggested four basic principles that make up the idea of stewardship. First, he brought out the point of divine ownership. In essence, God owns everything. The psalmist declared, "The earth is the Lord's, and all its fulness, the world and those who dwell therein" (Psalm 24:1).

Second, stewardship involves human endowment. Since it all belongs to God, whatever we have has been entrusted to us. To some He gives more, to others less (Matthew 25:14-15).

Stewardship requires faithful administration. What God has entrusted to us belongs to Him and He expects us to be faithful stewards of it. Paul was entrusted with the mystery of God and said, "…it is required in stewards that one be found faithful" (1 Corinthians 4:1-2).

Finally, an inevitable accounting will take place. In the parable of the talents, each man was held accountable to God for the way he handled God's possessions.

How does all of this tie in? As long as we deceive ourselves by playing the blame game, refusing to recognize our accountability to God, we will never effectively cope with our problems. We will always view the solution as existing outside of ourselves; as someone else's problem. If I have a behavioral problem, but continually blame you for the way I act, all I can do is wait for you to change before I can get my act together. Which means I must put my life on hold until you start taking responsible steps of action to change things. But the minute I assume the responsibility for my own actions I no longer need to wait for you.

So why do people act the way they do? What causes parents to abuse their children? Why do some practice homosexuality? What makes some people so mean and hard to get along with? Is there a cause-and-effect relationship between how people are treated and the way they act?

Please do not misunderstand me! I am not saying that evil influences have no part in the problem or the blame. They do! And those exerting the evil influence will give an account to God for that influence. What I am saying is this: each party involved will be held accountable for how they contribute to the problem. The one with the evil influence is responsible for his actions. The one whose behavior is contrary to God's will is responsible for having violated the Divine will.

Much of the confusion in the area of responsibility stems from confusing causes with their effects. Many are comfortably and willingly led to believe that they are not accountable or responsible for their quirky (sinful) behavior. They are led to believe that their mother or father, or some offender in the past, is solely responsible and that they cannot help themselves or keep from behaving in some abnormal (sinful) way.

I find a study of the Kings of Israel and Judah very

enlightening on this subject. For example, Ahab's life is summed up in these words: he "did that which was evil in the sight of Jehovah above all that were before him" (1 Kings 16:30). Ahab married a wicked woman named Jezebel, who happened to be a foreigner. [Marrying foreigners was against the Law of God (Exodus 34:12-17.)] Together, they raised a daughter named Athaliah. Athaliah led her son, Ahaziah, to walk after the wicked ways of her father, Ahab. (See 1 Kings 22:51-53). So we have wicked parents giving birth to a daughter who became wicked, who gave birth to a son who walked after both generations of wickedness.

There was another king named Ahaz who "did not do what was right in the sight of the Lord his God" (2 Kings 16:2). He was an idolater who caused his son to pass through the fire, according to the abominations of the nations. This was explicitly forbidden by the Law (Deuteronomy 12:31), and could easily be classified as child abuse or endangerment. This wicked king had a good son named Hezekiah (See 2 Kings 18:1-8). Unlike our first example, Hezekiah did not follow in his father's footsteps.

This same good man Hezekiah, had a son named Manasseh. Hezekiah was a good man, but Manasseh, his son, lived an evil life like his grandfather. He reinstituted idol worship by rebuilding the places of false worship that his father had torn down, and practiced every kind of abominable thing that accompanied such. Here we have an example of a good man whose son did what was evil in spite of the good influence of his father's life.

In the New Testament, we read of Timothy and the upbringing he received from his grandmother Lois and his mother

Eunice. These two godly women trained Timothy from his infancy in the sacred writings that were able to make him wise unto salvation. The Lord used Timothy in a mighty way as a co-worker of the apostle Paul. So, in our final example, we have a godly grandmother and mother training their son up in the way he should go, and he was faithful to that way.

Here is what we have so far:

- A wicked man married a wicked woman, who raised a wicked daughter, who gave birth to a man who lived a wicked life.

- In the second case, we have a wicked man whose son lived a life of honor and faithful obedience to God.

- In the third, a good and faithful man had a son who ended up doing that which was evil in the sight of God till the day he died.

- Finally, we see the influence of two faithful women on a young man to which two letters of the New Testament are written.

Is there a pattern? What are we to make of it all? Do evil parents guarantee evil children as an outcome? Do good parents always produce faithful children?

I have brought you through all of this to demonstrate that the bottom line in understanding the behavior of anyone is CHOICE. At some point in time each one of the Bible characters I have alluded to made some kind of choice—most likely a string of choices. Those choices then seemed to characterize each one of them as good or evil, but the choice was up to them as individuals.

We all make wrong choices for a number of reasons. It may be ignorance. Solomon said, "There is a way that seems right to a man, but its end is the way of death" (Proverbs 14:12). We may have been beguiled by the smooth and fair speech of others (Romans 16:17). We may be deceived like Eve. Note that Eve was not let off the hook because she was deceived; nor was Satan; nor was Adam. They all suffered consequences for their part in the fall. (See Genesis 3:14-19.) But much of the time we make wrong choices because we do not choose to do better. The lust of the flesh, the lust of the eye, and the pride of life draw us away, and we make wrong choices. Why? Simply because we choose to. Here is where the buck stops.

I would venture to say that the power of choice is one of the greatest freedoms God has given us. We have the freedom to choose life and what is good, or we can choose to destroy our lives and help to destroy the lives of others. So, with the freedom of choice comes much of responsibility!

> Free will is what has made evil possible. Why, then did God give free will? Because free will, though it makes evil possible, is also the only thing that makes possible any love or goodness or joy worth having. — C. S. Lewis

Life is given to us by God. It is given to us on loan. And we must learn to be a faithful steward of it, having been created as image-bearers of God (that is, created in His image). We must live our lives with the realization that one day we will all give an account to God for the choices we make; for the way we have behaved (Romans 14:12; 2 Corinthians 5:10).

If we reject the basic affirmation of this chapter, then we will not take responsibility for our own action and we will do nothing to effectively cope with the problems we face. Far too often we want to blame others for our misbehavior. But the fact is, even though others may have influenced us, we are still accomplices in the crime. We are responsible and accountable to God and others for our actions.

ACCOUNTABILITY WORKSHEET

One of the easiest things for us to do is point the finger of blame at someone else where our behavior is concerned..

Consider how the following characters illustrate man's tendency to either cover up the wrong he has done or to shift the finger of blame to someone, or something, other than himself.

1. Genesis 3:1-21

   a. Who did Adam blame?

   b. Who did Eve Blame?

   c. How effective was Adam and Eve's attempt to shift the responsibility of their action to another?

2. Exodus 32:1-24

   a. Who made the request for gods to be made?

   b. What role did Aaron play?

   c. When Moses returned from the mount and saw the golden calves what did he do with them?

   d. How did Aaron excuse himself and distance himself from

the "evil" people? (Exodus 32:21-24).

   e. How convincing was Aaron's response with you?

3. 1 Samuel 15

   a. When Samuel confronted Saul concerning his disobedience, what excuse did Saul offer? (1 Samuel 15:15ff).

   b. Did Saul take part with the people in disobeying God? (1 Samuel 15:9).

   c. How effective was Saul's seemingly pious excuse in justifying his disobedience to God?

Consider this positive example:

1. 2 Samuel 11-12

   a. How did King David initially try to hide his sin?

   b. When Nathan the prophet confronted David with his "hypothetical" case and then said, "You are the man," what did David say? (2 Samuel 12:13).

THINK ABOUT IT

1. What evil influences have there been in your life?

2. What part have you played - what decisions have you made - concerning your own behavior?

3. How effective do you think shifting the responsibility for your actions to someone else has been in helping you to cope effectively with your problem(s).

4. Why do we try to excuse ourselves of wrongdoing and

unacceptable behavior?

a. Pride

b. Denial

c. Embarrassment

d. Shame

e. Discomfort

5. What excuse have you offered to God and to others, perhaps even to yourself, for your behavior?

Perhaps you have been hurt, offended or sinned against, only to have the perpetrator shift the responsibility for his misconduct on someone or something else, and then offer some lame excuse for his action. Did that not add insult to injury? Did it not make you feel worse than the initial crime committed against you?

We have all heard some sorry excuses, and have been upset or disturbed by them. Just imagine how much our excuses must grieve God!

What can you do to better manage your life in the area of responsibility?

READ AND MEDITATE

1. Psalm 139

8

HONESTY

*Honesty—such a lonely word, everyone is so untrue. Honesty is
hardly ever heard, but mostly what I need from you.*

—Billy Joel

Two of the highest hurdles to jump in coping with problems
are humility and honesty. Learning to accept the truth about
us can be a big pill to swallow. That is why humility plays such an
important part in being honest.

In Jeremiah's day, the Lord said,

> The heart is deceitful above all things, and desperately wicked; Who can
> know it? I, the Lord, search the heart, I test the mind, even to give every
> man according to his ways, and according to the fruit of his doings"
> (Jeremiah 17:9-10).

One of the deceptive elements of the heart is its tendency to
deny there is a problem. For example, the writing workbook for

Adult Children of Alcoholics (ACA) identifies seven forms of denial (Workbook 1989, p. 28):

- Simple Denial: Pretending that something does not exist when it really does (e.g., discounting physical symptoms that may indicate the presence of problems).

- Minimizing: Being willing to acknowledge a problem, but unwilling to see its severity (e.g., admitting to estrangement in a relationship when in fact there is overt infidelity).

- Blaming: Blaming someone else for causing the problem: the behavior is not denied, but its cause is someone else's fault (e.g., blaming your parents for your current inappropriate behavior).

- Excusing: Offering excuses, alibis, justifications, and other explanations for our own or others' behavior (e.g., calling in sick for a partner when the actual cause of the absence is drunkenness).

- Generalizing: Dealing with problems on a general level, but avoiding personal and emotional awareness of the situation or conditions (e.g., sympathizing with a friend's flu symptoms when you know chemical dependency is the underlying cause of the problem).

- Dodging: Changing the subject to avoid threatening topics (e.g., becoming adept at "small talk").

- Attacking: Becoming angry and irritable when reference is made to the existing condition, thus avoiding the issue (e.g., being unwilling to share your feelings).

We need to acknowledge that we are naked before God and that our hearts are corrupt. Jeremiah reminds us of this corruption (Jeremiah 17:9). This being the case, how could we ever pretend that no one knows what we are doing? No secret of the heart can be concealed from Him. King David prayed:

Search me, O God, and know my heart;

Try me, and know my anxieties;
And see if there is any wicked way in me,
And lead me in the way everlasting (Psalm 139:23-24).

A person would need to have a very honest relationship with God before he would ever invite Him to search his private thought life. David also acknowledged the fact that nothing escapes God's sight:

If I say, "Surely the darkness shall fall on me,"
Even the night shall be light about me;
Indeed, the darkness shall not hide from You,
But the night shines as the day;
The darkness and the light are both alike to You (Ps. 139:11-12).

Look back at that statement again. David argues that he could hypothetically say, "Surely the darkness shall fall on me, even the night shall be light about me" as if to say that whatever evil he may do will not be seen by God under the cover of darkness. But the truth is, even the darkness cannot hide him. Where God is concerned, the night shines as the day. "The darkness and the light are both alike to You."

Paul informs us: "Some men's sins are clearly evident, preceding them to judgment, but those of some men follow later. Likewise, the good works of some are clearly evident, and those that are otherwise cannot be hidden" (1 Timothy 5:24, 25). You and I do not see everything that goes on because not everything is evident. But sins, as well as good works, will follow a man to judgment whether they are evident to us or not, if not covered by the blood of Jesus. God "will judge the secrets of men by Jesus Christ, according to my gospel" (Romans 2:16).

In an earlier chapter, we learned that God's Word is penetrating. It is able to discern the thoughts and intents of the heart (Hebrews 4:12). "And there is no creature hidden from His sight, but all things are naked and open to the eyes of Him to whom we must give account" (4:13). In fact, James compared God's Word to a mirror into which many look and from which they walk away, forgetting what manner of man they are (James 1:22-24). If we can learn to hold that mirror steady before us, perhaps it will keep us honest.

In the popular Twelve Step Program, the fourth of those twelve steps is perhaps one of the most challenging. It calls upon its practitioners to make a searching and fearless moral inventory of oneself. This is good advice, providing we use the word of God as our standard in the assessment. In order to effectively cope with life, everything we do and think must be measured by God! Saturating our minds with God's Word, coupled with an honest heart, God can then perform the inventory and identify where we are lacking so we can change where necessary.

Leaving God's Word out of the "searching and fearless inventory" leads to foolishness. In fact, this happened to be one of the more difficult disciplines for me to engage in when I was young in Christ. When I read passages like Romans 3:10 - "There is none righteous no not one," I added "except Steve Lloyd." I thought I was a pretty nice guy. I didn't carouse with the girls. I didn't drink. I didn't smoke. I didn't use drugs. So, compared to so many others, I "honestly" looked pretty good to myself.

It was only when I began reading the Bible that I realized as long as I compared myself with others I would look pretty good.

(By the way, Paul says this is a foolish standard of judgment, 2 Corinthians 10:12.) But when I began comparing myself with the holy and righteous standard established by God and exemplified in His Son, I realized I needed to strike the exception clause I had added to Romans 3:10. I had trusted in my own relative "goodness" for a right standing with God.

The searching and fearless moral inventory must be conducted while standing unflinchingly in front of the mirror of God's discerning Word. If we guard against having a deceitful and exceedingly corrupt heart when we meditate on the Scriptures, God will make the searching moral inventory of our life, and this will lead to change.

> The characters in the Gospel accounts "...are sketched with sure strokes, but not so fully as to preclude our identifying ourselves with them. Their faces are never so completely drawn that we cannot place our own heads on their shoulders: we could be blind man, neighbor, parent, or Pharisee and it can be instructive for us to assume each role in turn as we read. — Roland Frye

In an earlier chapter, we noted how important attitude is, especially humility. This requires poverty of spirit (Matthew 5:3). Responsible steps of action that will reap the changes necessary for us to effectively cope with the issue of our life also require honesty.

THE PLACE OF PRAYER

In making a searching and fearless moral inventory, God's Word is indispensable. To be added to this inventory is prayer.

Robert Milligan wrote several articles on the subject of prayer back in the mid-1800's for the Millennial Harbinger. These articles were later published in a small book titled, *A Brief Treatise on Prayer*. In discussing Jesus' instruction on going to our closet to pray in the Sermon on the Mount, Robert Milligan wrote:

> There is no other place beneath the heavens that is so favorable for the legitimate exercise of our moral faculties. Even in the religious assembly, the attention is often arrested and the heart made to wander by some improper display of the lusts of the flesh, the lusts of the eye, and the pride of life. But from the closet all such evil influences are excluded. There is no motive to deceive, or to make a vain display of our persons, our dress, and our good works. But there the mind turns in upon itself. There the conscience is awakened; there we see ourselves in the light of heaven. And there, under the deep, solemn conviction that we are on holy ground, and that the eye of God is upon us, we are almost compelled to be humble, to repent of our sins, to forgive our enemies, to sympathize with the afflicted, to adore our Creator, to love our Redeemer, and to exercise all the powers of our souls in harmony with the will of God (Milligan 1966, p. 16).

When you are alone before the throne of grace with "no motive to deceive, or to make a vain display of our person, our dress, and our good works" we are practically compelled to recognize that our soul is naked and laid open before God. What else can we do but be honest? We would all do well to incorporate "closet time" into our schedules.

HONESTY WORKSHEET

The Fourth Step of the famous Twelve Step Program calls on its practitioners to make a searching and fearless moral inventory of oneself. According to those who have attended such workshops this inventory is made up strictly of things that bother the individual personally. I would like to take this exercise one step further. If we saturate our minds with God's Word, and couple that with an honest heart, God can then perform the inventory with His Word and identify the areas of our life we need to change - which will not only include areas that bother us, but areas that bother God also.

THINK ABOUT IT

1. What reaction do you get in knowing that there is nothing you can hide from God?

2. Why do you suppose you have that reaction(s)?

3. What is it that permitted King David to so openly invite God to try him and to know his thoughts? (Psalm 139)

4. Are there areas of your life that you do not believe you have been honest about - if so, what are they?

   a. What has hindered you from being honest with yourself in these areas?

   b. What would it take for you to invite God to search your private thought-life?

5. Read Matthew 6:5-15.

   a. Look back at Matthew 6:1 for the focus of the verses you just read. What does it say?

   b. How did the Pharisees pray, and for what purpose did they pray in that way?

   c. In contrast, how are we instructed to pray?

   d. Look back at Robert Milligan's statement concerning "closet prayers" and identify some of the benefits of such a prayer.

e. Is there anything that stands in the way of your desire to be with God?

READ AND MEDITATE

1. Psalm 139

2. Matthew 6:5-15

9

CHANGE

Now I rejoice, not that you were made sorry, but that your sorrow led to
repentance. For you were made sorry in a godly manner, that you might
suffer loss from us in nothing. For godly sorrow produces repentance leading
to salvation not to be regretted; but the sorrow of the world produces death.

—Paul

Solomon hammers home the point that true and lasting
enjoyment is a gift from the hand of God.

> There is nothing better for a man than that he should eat and drink, and
> that his soul should enjoy good in his labor. This also, I saw, was from
> the hand of God. For who can eat, or who can have enjoyment, more
> than I? For God gives wisdom and knowledge and joy to a man who is
> good in His sight; but to the sinner He gives the work of gathering and
> collecting, that he may give to him who is good before God. This also is
> vanity and grasping for the wind (Ecclesiastes 2:24-26).

Some suggest that when Solomon said, "For who can eat, or
who can have enjoyment, more than I?" that the phrase "more

99

than I" could also be translated "apart from Him." The point is, who can even eat or enjoy life apart from God? Good question!

> Here is what I have seen: It is good and fitting for one to eat and drink, and to enjoy the good of all his labor in which he toils under the sun all the days of his life which God gives him; for it is his heritage. As for every man to whom God has given riches and wealth, and given him power to eat of it, to receive his heritage and rejoice in his labor - this is the gift of God. For he will not dwell unduly on the days of his life, because God keeps him busy with the joy of his heart (Ecclesiastes 5:18-20; also see 8:15 & 9:7-10).

In order to obtain the kind of happiness and goodness here spoken of, change is required. Counseling is about change. Preaching, in part, is about change.

We have already discovered that sin is at the root of most of our problems; that it disrupts our fellowship with God and, consequently, our very lives. False beliefs also function as foils to what would otherwise be a good life. Change is required, and the kind of change we will be addressing as it relates to many of the problems we face is called "repentance" in the Bible. Repentance is brought about by the right kind of sorrow.

There are two kinds of sorrow. Paul wrote, "For godly sorrow produces repentance to salvation, not to be regretted; but the sorrow of the world produces death" (2 Corinthians 7:10). For the church in Corinth, "godly sorrow" produced a number of good things: an earnest care, a clearing of themselves, fear, longing, and zeal (7:11).

The wise King Solomon said:

> It is better to go to the house of mourning

Than to go to the house of feasting,
For that is the end of all men;
And the living will take it to heart.
Sorrow is better than laughter,
For by a sad countenance the heart is made better.
The heart of the wise is in the house of mourning,
But the heart of fools is in the house of mirth (Ecclesiastes 7:2-4).

Solomon is affirming that it is more profitable to go to a funeral than to a party because funerals reminds us all that death is the end of us all. Being reminded of this will provoke us to adjust our lives with that end in mind.

Forgetting to contemplate the outcome of a thing can be a fatal move on our part. For example, the Psalmist, Asaph, said that his steps had almost slipped out from under him when he considered the prosperity of the wicked. He had even entertained the idea that he had cleansed his hands before God in vain. All of it was too painful for him to bear until he went into the sanctuary of God "and considered their latter end" (Psalm 73:17, ASV). It was only when he considered the ultimate end of the wicked who prospered in the material things of this life that he realized it was really the feet of those he envied that were on slippery ground. Remembering their latter end provoked an important change in him.

A popular bumper sticker reads: "The one who dies with the most toys wins." But an amended sticker reads: "The one who dies with the most toys still dies." That is what Asaph discovered when he went into the sanctuary of God and considered the latter end of the wicked.

Jeremiah informs us that one of the causes of Judah's demise at the hand of Nebuchadnezzar, king of Babylon, was that "she remembered not her latter end" (Lamentations 1:9). God had told Israel centuries earlier, back in the days of Moses, that if they ever became disobedient to Him they would lose their privileged status in the Promised Land. One writer summarizes Judah's sad condition in these words:

> Moreover all the leaders of the priests and the people transgressed more and more, according to all the abominations of the nations, and defiled the house of the Lord which He had consecrated in Jerusalem. And the Lord God of their fathers sent warnings to them by His messengers, rising up early and sending them, because He had compassion on His people and on His dwelling place. But they mocked the messengers of God, despised His words, and scoffed at His prophets, until the wrath of the Lord arose against His people, till there was no remedy. Therefore he brought against them the king of the Chaldeans, who killed their young men with the sword in the house of their sanctuary, and had no compassion on young man or virgin, on the aged or the weak; He gave them all into his hand (2 Chronicles 36:14-17).

The Book of Lamentations is comprised of five funeral dirges that mourn the demise of Judah's destruction. Perhaps if she had kept her latter end in mind, it would have prompted her to remain faithful.

The last principle we discussed addressed the issue of honesty. If we are honest with ourselves and fearlessly permit God to make a searching moral inventory of our lives, it should humble us. It should cause each of us to acknowledge that we are destitute in spirit and in desperate need of God. I seriously doubt that the right frame of mind is present if we do not recognize how desperate a condition we are in apart from Him.

Phil Donahue asked his TV guest, who by the way had five wives, "If God said polygamy was wrong would you stop practicing polygamy?" The guest with the five wives said, "Oh, I'd change gods."

The first beatitude in the Sermon on the Mount is: "Blessed are the poor in spirit: for theirs is the kingdom of heaven" (Matthew 5:3). The second of those beatitudes flows naturally from the first: "Blessed are they that mourn: for they shall be comforted" (5:4). The mourning referred to here is caused by a contemplation of sin; our own sin and the sins of the world, and may include sickness and suffering, etc.

James concurs:

> Lament and mourn and weep! Let your laughter be turned to mourning and your joy to gloom. Humble yourselves in the sight of the Lord, and He will lift you up (4:9-10). (James draws a connection between the first two beatitudes in these remarks.)

Blessed mourning produces a glad heart and is rewarded with comfort from the Lord.

To take this one step further, the house of mourning that Solomon spoke of is the only place we can go that has the power to motivate us to make the necessary changes in our life.

FEAR OF CHANGE

Change can be a frightening thing. Even when the change we consider is for the better, it can be frightening. And because change, even for the better, is frightening many do whatever they can to avoid it. When life becomes unmanageable and we are forced to face it, it is no longer something that we can put on the back burner or sweep under the rug.

A number of years ago, I visited with a woman who had been molested by her father as a young girl and gang-raped on the streets of her own home town.

To see what foundation needed to be built in our time together I asked her if she had any personal convictions about whether there was a God. At first she said she did not believe God existed. Then she changed her answer and said, "It's not that I don't believe there is a God. It's just that I hate Him for letting that happen to me."

We met, sporadically, for the next year and a half. I am still convinced that the Scriptures would have helped her. I am persuaded that she even saw in them the potential for making a beneficial difference. But she never enacted any changes in her life.

She is a prime example of someone learning what the Bible teaches, but not necessarily liking what they hear. Consequently no divinely guided changes were enacted in her life. I think I am safe in saying that where there is no change there is no hope. Rather than turn to God and rely on His wisdom for help, she turned to illicit drugs and alcohol to anesthetize the pain in her life.

I was asked to visit her in a sanitarium years after our time together. I asked her if she had discussed with her doctor the things she had told me so many years ago. She gave me a puzzled look and asked, "What things?" I cautiously reminded her of a few things to see how she would react. A tear rolled down her emotionless face and she denied ever having said those things. She treated those horrible events as if they had never happened.

COPING: A BIBLICAL APPROACH

When problems become unmanageable to the extent that we can no longer avoid them we must cry out to God for help.

Interestingly enough, with reference to life becoming unmanageable, the third beatitude of our Lord is, "Blessed are the meek" (Matthew 5:5). To be meek is to be *tame* or *under control*. This is important to know when life is out of control. The time is right for change when we humble ourselves and learn to mourn over our condition. At that point, and only at that point, will we be ready to turn over the controls to God. Since nothing we do independent from God can ever affect lasting benefits, the wise course for us is to place ourselves under His control.

We challenge God for control of our lives. It is something we don't give up without a fight. We simply do not like being told what to do. The apostle Paul refers to the whole issue of control as a struggle between the Spirit and the flesh. He said, "For the flesh lusts against the Spirit, and the Spirit against the flesh; and these are contrary to one another; so that you do not do the things that you wish" (Galatians 5:17). To be under the control of the Spirit, one must make the conscious decision to die to the things of the flesh and to walk according to the guidance of the Spirit.

A MEAN BETWEEN EXTREMES

Aristotle, in *Nicomachean Ethics*, argues that virtues are the means between extremes. For example, the mean between rashness and cowardice is courage. Courage is a virtue. A virtue is a right desire.

Meekness is a mean between two extremes. One extreme is uncontrolled rage; the other is passive non-anger. A meek person does not abandon himself to rage nor does he seek to anesthetize himself beyond feeling. This virtue requires control and control requires change. And change begins with mourning.

Mortimer Adler, a popular writer in philosophy today, explains in one of his autobiographies why he had not committed himself to the God he had philosophically proven to exist. He writes, it

>...would require a radical change in my life, a basic alteration in the direction of my day-to-day choices as well as in the ultimate objectives to be sought or hoped for. I have all too clear and too detailed an understanding of moral theology to fool myself on that score. The simple truth of the matter is that I did not wish to live up to being a genuinely religious person. I could not bring myself to will what I ought to will for my whole future if I were to resolve my will, at a particular moment, with regard to religious conversion.

When we have implemented the right kind of change (repentance) for the right reasons (godly sorrow) God is able to work in us! If we want the abundant life that Jesus promised His sheep (John 10:10), we must submit ourselves to Him in humility. Through submission to His word our lives will be transformed (changed) and the abundant life promised will be supplied.

If you fear change for the better, let me close by asking you to consider these questions: What has sin ever done for you? Where are you going with your present course of action?

CONSIDER

Jesus, in His Good Shepherd discourse, said, "I have come that they may have life, and that they may have it more abundantly" (John 10:10). When we live our lives to their capacity, God is glorified. When people see "love, joy, peace, longsuffering, kindness, goodness, faithfulness, gentleness and self-control" (Galatians 5:22) in us, they will say, "Let us go with you, for we have heard that God is with you" (Zechariah 8:23). They will see that God is with us by the fruit produced in our lives.

Now, if our lives do not bear the fruit of the Spirit at least two things will result. First of all, we will not bring honor to God. When the necessary changes have occurred in us, people will see it and say, "Look what great good God has done in this person's life." If these qualities are absent, then our lives, to the contrary, give occasion for the enemies of God to speak evil of Him. "Look at him or her. He claims to be a Christian. Hah! What has God done for him? He's the same miserable guy he's always been."

Which leads me to my next point. If our lives are all that they could be, others will be attracted to them and desire what we have. Who in their right mind would "convert" from one miserable burdened existence to another miserable burdened existence? If our lives are not what they ought to be, how effective an appeal do you suppose we can make to win others to Christ? "Hey, why don't you leave that miserable life you lead and come be miserable with me?" Is that what we are inviting others to do?

The point is: change is required. As you will see, change involves effort, temporary discomfort, and trust in God.

CHANGE WORKSHEET

Effective change will involve one or more of the following:

- effort

- temporary discomfort

- trust in God

Because we have settled into a behavior—even harmful behavior—it will require effort to change. Changing from one kind of behavior to another may involve temporary discomfort. That's because it requires effort. We must think about what we are doing. (One man said, "There is no expedient to which a man will not go to avoid the real labor of thinking.") We must believe that God knows what is best for us, and forsake the unprofitable path we have been traveling.

Sometimes we can get so used to a bad thing that we get comfortable, even in the most undesirable of circumstances, and do not want to go to the trouble involved in changing our lives for the better.

Consider the Israelites as they were delivered from Egyptian bondage. After deliverance from the oppressive hand of the Egyptian Empire, Israel asked Moses, "Why have you brought us out?" Back in Egypt they were crying out to God for deliverance. God saw their "misery." He heard their "crying." He was concerned about their "suffering." So he delivered them. Compare Exodus 14:11 with Exodus 3:7ff.

THINK ABOUT IT

1. What do you need to change in your life?

2. Do you feel intimidated by the thought of changing in any of these areas? What would change involve?

3. How have you dealt with these issues in the past?

4. How profitable was your handling of these issues?

5. What does the Bible have to say concerning the issues you confront?

6. Some people do not believe that change is possible. Consider the following passages:

    a. 1 Corinthians 6:9-11

    b. 2 Peter 2:20

    c. Colossians 3:1-17

    d. Ephesians 4:17-32

7. What is the difference between self-pity and mourning over sin? The dynamics involved in change are directly connected to what we covered under the principles of success. The relationship between meditating on God's Word and change was brought out in chapter 5.

READ AND MEDITATE

1. Psalm 119 (look back at the notes you made on this Psalm in Chapter 5.)

2. Romans 12:1-2

3. 2 Corinthians 7:10

10

FORGIVENESS

Guilt, the gift that keeps on giving. —Garrison Keillor

Jesus, the Master Teacher, had a powerful way of getting a point across by means of telling the world's greatest short stories. One of the most well known of those stories is commonly called "The Parable of the Prodigal Son."

The story is found in Luke 15, and is preceded by two other parables that teach the same basic thing. All three stories share the same structure:

- something/someone is lost

- something/someone is found

- there is rejoicing over finding what was lost.

The first parable could be titled "The Lost Sheep." When the lost sheep is found, people are called together to rejoice over its restoration to the fold, and Jesus says, "I say to you that likewise there will be more joy in heaven over one sinner who repents than over ninety-nine just persons who need no repentance" (15:7).

The second parable could be titled "The Lost Coin." When the woman who lost the coin finds it she rejoices, and Jesus says, "Likewise, I say to you, there is joy in the presence of the angels of God over one sinner who repents" (15:10).

In keeping with the first two titles, the third parable we could call "The Lost Son." The lost son has been dubbed the "prodigal" son for good reason. The word "prodigal" means "recklessly wasteful; extravagant." When the younger son took his portion of his father's substance, Jesus said he "wasted his possessions with prodigal living" (15:13). When the wasteful son returned home, his father said, "This my son was dead, and is alive again; he was lost and is found" (15:24). And having been found, the father calls his servants to join him in his joy.

There are several characters in the story itself. Jesus begins the story by saying, "A certain man had two sons." These are the primary characters around which Jesus presents His lesson. The younger son says to his father, "Father give me the portion of goods that fall to me." The father divided his living between his two sons.

What the younger son asked for was equivalent to wishing his father were dead. So his request was both bold and cold. For what did this younger boy make such a request? It was to waste his substance with riotous living. He was a first century party animal. The NIV says he "squandered his wealth in wild living." Here we have a young man implying a desire for the death of his father to finance him in the wild life.

The prodigal son faced many problems. First of all, he positioned himself far away from home. Jesus said, he "took his journey into a far country." Second, he depleted his funds. "He wasted his funds." Third, as if depleting his funds was not bad enough, they were spent in riotous living. Later, the older son would accuse him of having devoured his father's substance with harlots (15:30). The fourth problem he faced was a mighty famine. After he had spent all, Jesus said, "there arose a severe famine in that land, and he began to be in want" (15:14). To make matters worse, especially for a Jew, the only work he could find was feeding loathsome swine in the field. He was so bad off that he would have gladly eaten the carob pods given to the hogs, but no one was so generous.

Then Jesus makes a curious statement characterizing this young man's change of heart. In this humiliating condition Jesus says of him, "he came to himself" as if to say that he finally came to his senses.

> But when he came to himself, he said, How many of my father's hired servants have bread enough and to spare, and I perish with hunger! I will arise and go to my father, and will say to him, Father, I have sinned against heaven and before you, and I am no longer worthy to be called your son. Make me like one of your hired servants. And he arose and came to his father (Luke 15:17-20).

The young prodigal had a change of heart.

What kind of father did he have? Jesus said, "But when he was still a great way off, his father saw him and had compassion, and ran and fell on his neck and kissed him" (15:20).

The son said to his father: "Father, I have sinned against heaven and in your sight, and am no longer worthy to be called your son" (15:21).

The father said to his servants,

Bring out the best robe and put it on him, and put a ring on his hand and sandals on his feet. And bring the fatted calf here and kill it, and let us eat and be merry; for this my son was dead and is alive again; he was lost and is found (15:22-24).

The father does not verbalize his forgiveness in so many words, but rather expresses it by embracing his son and putting a robe, ring, and shoes on him, and killing the fatted calf.

Then there is the older brother, who thought he was not getting a fair shake in the whole matter. (READ 15:25-32.)

Jesus paints a very realistic picture of what happens in families. With the older son, Jesus turns the parable into an attack on the Pharisees and scribes in his audience (15:1, 2). While the older son should have been rejoicing with his father, he was, instead, focusing on things his father had not done for him.

In some of Jesus' parables he calls for his hearers to make a judgment on the characters in the parable, in this one he leaves them to reach their own conclusions. His rebuke of the Pharisees and scribes is implied.

In essence there are three themes in the parable: redemption, forgiveness, and jealousy. The father receives his younger son with forgiveness. The older son is enraged with jealousy and envy, and even scolds his father for so openly accepting his younger son home. As it relates to the setting in which it was told, we see Jesus receiving and eating with the publicans and sinners. Is it not ironic that the Pharisees and scribes could probably relate to the joy of finding a lost sheep or lost coin more so than they could the restoration of a sinner?!

Perhaps the application of this parable for us today can be found by examining the ways in which the wayward son was received. The father "…when he was still a great way off, …saw him and had compassion, and ran and fell on his neck and kissed him" (15:20). The father had a great deal he could have held against his son, but no evidence of a grudge is to be found in the story. In fact, the father garbs his son with the best robe, a ring, and shoes, and had the fatted calf killed. How did the father view his son's return? "…my son was dead and is alive again; he was lost and is found."

In the older son, we see a satiric attack on the scribes and Pharisees. In their pride and arrogance, they looked down on the sinners and publicans; and in this account, they looked down on Jesus for receiving them and eating with them.

Jesus' subtle attack on their attitude implies that there is probably nothing a "sinner or publican" could do to get into the "good graces" of the Pharisees. So Jesus attacks these self-righteous men for their smug and prejudicial attitudes.

Of the two attitudes expressed toward the penitent son, our Lord wants us to respond like the father in the story. It is how our Father of heaven responds. It is how Jesus responded. It is how we should respond.

There are examples in the church where someone similar to the younger son has "come home" but was not welcomed by an "older brother" only to leave discouraged and with nowhere else to turn. May we all act more like the father in Jesus' masterful story, and much less like the older brother when we are faced with a "younger brother" who was dead, but now alive; lost, but found.

Perhaps you have been living in that far country. If you have left the Lord, you need to return with the same spirit as the younger son.

GOD'S NATURE TO FORGIVE

Many of our problems center around learning how to properly relate to God. If we harbor false concepts of God, we will operate on false concepts of how He relates to us. For instance, if we believe that God requires flawless perfection from us before He will care for us or love us, we are doomed to misery and despair. Because we have all fallen short of His glory, we could never become the recipients of His care or His love if the above was true.

The very word "gospel" means "good news." But how good would the news be if perfection were required of us for justification?

Roy Lanier Sr., a respected Bible scholar, once wrote:

> ...in the gospel it is revealed that this justification from faith is 'unto faith.' By this Paul means that the 'good news' is that the ungodly may have justification, a right standing with God, on the condition of faith in Jesus Christ, and this revelation is made in order to induce men to believe in, put their trust in, Jesus Christ as the Son of God. Says some

one, I have good news for you. Well, what is it? I ask. He says, you can have a right standing with God if you will never commit another sin. Would that be good news to you? It is not to me. But, if some one says he has good news for me and tells me that I can have a right standing, justification, from God on the condition that I put my trust in Jesus who loved me so much that he died to make my salvation possible, that will prompt me to believe on Christ Jesus that I might be justified by faith and not by good works.

Many people in the world and in the church live with false concepts of God. And they live their lives and base their decisions in light of these false concepts.

We should take seriously the responsibility of meditating on God's Word continually, allowing Him to tell us what He is like. We must consider our pursuit of God as a lifelong one, ever learning and reminding ourselves of God's true nature and our own.

How can a person be certain God has forgiven him? The forgiveness of sins is inseparably tied in with the blood of Christ. The writer of Hebrews informs us that "without the shedding of blood there is no remission" (Hebrews 9:22). Yet, the remission of sins is received when a person is baptized into Christ. Consider these passages:

- Peter said to the crowd at Pentecost: "Repent, and let every one of you be baptized in the name of Jesus Christ for the remission of sins; and you shall receive the gift of the Holy Spirit" (Acts 2:38).

- Paul was told by Ananias: "And now why are you waiting? Arise and be baptized, and wash away your sins, calling on the name of the Lord" (Acts 22:16)

- As recorded in Matthew's account of the Great Commission Jesus said, "All authority has been given to Me in heaven and on earth. Go therefore and make disciples of all the nations, baptizing them in the name of the Father and of the Son and of the Holy Spirit, teaching them to observe all things that I have commanded you; and lo, I am with you always, even to the end of the age" (Matthew 28:18-20).

- As recorded in Mark's account, Jesus said: "Go into all the world and preach the gospel to every creature. He who believes and is baptized will be saved; but he who does not believe will be condemned" (Mark 16:15-16).

The apostle Paul argued that when a person is baptized they are baptized into Christ's death. Jesus shed His blood in his death. So when we are baptized, we actually receive the benefits of the blood Jesus shed in death. Paul also argues that we reenact the death, burial, and resurrection in baptism. We die to sin, we are buried with Him in baptism, and are raised to walk in newness of life. (Study Romans 6.)

God commended His love toward us in that while we were yet sinners Christ died for us (Romans 5:8). He so loved the world that He gave is only-begotten Son for the sins of the world (John 3:16). God is love (1 John 4:8, 16). He is love and stands ready to forgive us as we repent.

CAUSES OF DOUBT
What are some of the causes of doubt concerning God's forgiveness?

Let me suggest first of all that there might be a lack of faith involved. If I believe that I have lived a life so corrupt that God cannot forgive me, and yet the Scriptures tell me He can, then I must decide who I am going to believe. The problem here is one of faith. Am I going to believe some notion I have concocted or am I going to believe God?

Another cause of doubt has already been mentioned above and that is false concepts of God. Some people tend to see God the same way they see their earthly fathers. They are not the same. Our earthly fathers may have been unreasonable and brutal and unfair. They may have made us believe that the only way we could ever deserve their love is to merit it by performing well in sports, in school, and keeping our rooms clean, etc. This whole mentality is many times superimposed on God, and people end up believing that the only way they could ever "deserve" God's love is by a flawless performance. If our lives were flawless, there would be no need for the Savior, Jesus Christ.

Some entertain doubts about being forgiven due to false concepts of God's love. They believe, though they may not have thought it through, that they must earn God's love by being perfect. We hear statements like, "I don't deserve God's love" and "How could God love me?" What people need to know is that God's very nature is to love, and that it is not something that can be earned or merited. We can either accept it or reject it. God already loves us, as demonstrated on the cross. What this frees us from is the belief that only by living a flawless life could God ever love us.

God's longsuffering with Paul is given as an example for those who later believe on Christ unto eternal life. Prior to his conversion, Paul was a blasphemer, a persecutor, and injurious to the church of Jesus Christ. He writes, "but I obtained mercy because I did it ignorantly in unbelief. And the grace of our Lord was exceedingly abundant, with faith and love which are in Christ

`-14). Paul said, "This is a faithful saying
ice, that Christ Jesus came into the
. whom I am chief" (1 Timothy 1:15). The
⌐ can forgive Paul, surely He can and will
.ough our obedience to the Gospel of His Son.

.other cause of doubt concerning God's forgiveness may
ɔtem from confusing forgiveness with remorse. While we may
have been forgiven, we should still feel remorse or regret for our
behavior.

Some forms of depression are caused by anger turned inward.
We may still feel some sense of anger toward ourselves for
wrongs we have committed in the past. However, remorse or
regret can be turned around to work for our good by motivating
us never to repeat wrong behavior. See 2 Corinthians 7:8-11
where Paul said godly sorrow works repentance unto salvation.

Perhaps another cause for doubt may be the fact that true
repentance has never occurred. It may be the case that we want
all of the benefits Christianity has to offer us, i.e., salvation,
forgiveness, access to God through Jesus Christ, etc., but it may
be the case that we do not want to mend or change our ways. If
an individual has not truly converted (changed) it should not be a
surprise if they do not "feel" forgiven. Paul wrote that the sorrow
of the world works death. This kind of sorrow is not accompanied
by forgiveness from God.

CONCLUDING REMARKS

The picture painted of God by the brush of holy men of old is that
He is love and stands ready to forgive us when we obey the
gospel, which involves repentance. It may be the case that you do

not think that God is able to forgive you. The apostle Paul offers us proof positive that God stands ready to forgive us. He is like the father in the parable of the prodigal son.

Causes of doubt may include:

• lack of faith

• false concepts of God

• confusion between forgiveness and remorse

• lack of genuine repentance

I hope that you will use this partial list to explore the reasons why you may have trouble believing that you are forgiven.

FORGIVENESS WORKSHEET

How we relate to God is of critical importance. How we relate to one another is a critical element as well. All sin is against God, but it may involve others. When we sin against one another we need to learn how to respond properly.

If I have sinned against you, it does not do merely to say, "I'm sorry." While this is an important thing to confess, I do not believe the offense has been absolved until we say to the party we have offended, "Will you forgive me?" These are four of the most important words we could utter to the one we have offended. If you don't believe me, think about the last time you were offended. If the offender came to you and said, 'Listen, if you have a problem with what I did, I'm sorry." How satisfied would you be? The offender has just offended you again by suggesting that you are still the one with the problem. Consider how much more satisfying it would be if that same individual were to have said, "I know what I did the other day was offensive to you. I am very sorry I offended you. Would you please forgive me?" Do you see the difference between the first and second statements?

If you are the offender, then you must approach the one you offended and ask for their forgiveness. But what if the offender refuses to forgive you when forgiveness is sought? Then the one offended is the one with the problem. His problem is then with God, Who will not forgive the unforgiving.

Consider the message expressed by the following passages:

1. Luke 15:11-32 (READ)

   a. What two reactions were there to the son who was dead and is alive again, and was lost and is found?

   b. Comparing these two reactions with the two categories of people referred to in Luke 15:1-2, how does this parable relate to the audience?

   c. Which character in the story ought we to be like?

2. Matthew 18:21-35 (READ)

   a. How much money did the servant of this story owe the king? What is that equivalent to today? (vs 24)

   b. How much did one of his fellow-servants owe him? What is that equivalent to today? (vs 28)

   c. What happened to the forgiven servant who did not, in turn, forgive others?

   d. What is the lesson Jesus wants us to learn? (vs 35)

Think about it

If an individual has sinned against us and they do not seek forgiveness, we are powerless to forgive. Many people think that we ought to forgive even those who do not seek it. Not even God forgives those who have not repented. Why should we hold ourselves accountable to forgive those God Himself has not forgiven?

Even though we are powerless to forgive until the offender repents, we are to stand ready to forgive like the father in the story of the lost son (Luke 15:11-32). Bitterness and malice in our hearts only hurts us.

1. Against whom have you committed an offense that you have not asked forgiveness?

2. Have you withheld your forgiveness from anyone who has repented of their actions toward you?

3. Why is asking for forgiveness and forgiving difficult at times?

4. What are some of the causes of doubt about being forgiven by God?

READ AND MEDITATE

1. 1 John 1:7-10

2. Psalm 32

3. Psalm 51

4. Psalm 103:12

5. Mark 16:15-16

6. Acts 2:37-42

7. Ephesians 2:1-10

11

ABSTINENCE

Here's to abstinence - as long as it's practiced in moderation. ——Reader's Digest

John was attracted to pornography when he was a teen. He was so hooked that he would steal magazines from the store to feed his mind with their off-limit pictures. Advertisements in other magazines were stimulating enough to set his mind meditating on shameful things. Billboards on the side of the freeway and T.V. commercials did nothing to help. John knew what he was doing was wrong and tried to eliminate pornography from his life, . . . but he kept a few magazines in his closet "just in case." Today's internet has become the avenue for the downfall for many men.

I have known people who wanted to quit smoking, but kept a carton of cigarettes in a kitchen cabinet just in case they were not able to make it through a day without one. The same could be said of people with alcohol and drug problems.

The principle we need to commit ourselves to is found in Romans 13:14. There Paul writes, "But put on the Lord Jesus Christ, and make no provision for the flesh, to fulfill its lust." He just exhorted the saints in Rome to cast off the works of darkness and to put on the whole armor of light: and to walk becomingly, as in the day. Then he elaborates on what he means by works of darkness.

> Let us walk properly, as in the day, not in revelry and drunkenness, not in licentiousness and lewdness, not in strife and envy. But put on the Lord Jesus Christ, and make no provision for the flesh, to fulfill its lusts (Romans 13:14).

The NIV renders the three couplets in this passage: "not in orgies and drunkenness, not in sexual immorality and debauchery, not in dissension and jealousy." How were they to avoid these enemies of the flesh? By putting on the Lord Jesus Christ, and by not making provision for the flesh to gratify its desires.

Anyone who keeps pornography around (or alcohol or drugs or whatever else may provide them an opportunity to stumble) is simply not engaged in a battle they expect to win. They are affording themselves opportunities to fail. An essential step in casting off the works of darkness is to avoid making provisions for the flesh.

In the Reader's Digest's "Toward More Picturesque Speech," I found this cheer: "Here's to abstinence—as long as it's practiced in moderation." This statement is designed to provoke a chuckle, but as you can see abstinence and moderation are contradictions in terms.

Jesus took the issue of abstinence seriously. So serious, in fact, that He advised us to pluck out the eye that looks upon a woman to lust after her and to cut off the hand that causes us to stumble and throw it away, "...for it is more profitable for you that one of your members perish, than for your whole body to be cast into hell" (Matthew 5:30b). In essence, Jesus is saying that we should eliminate from our lives anything that could easily become a source of temptation (Romans 13:14).

WALKING AFTER THE SPIRIT

One of the greatest battles fought every day goes on inside each one of us. It is the battle of the flesh against the Spirit, and the Spirit against the flesh. Paul wrote, "Walk by the Spirit, and ye shall not fulfill the lust of the flesh" (Galatians 5:16). The reason this battle is such a crucial one is that if the flesh wins out condemnation is the reward. They that practice the works of the flesh shall not inherit the kingdom of God.

In Galatians Chapter 5, Paul writes, "For the flesh lusts against the Spirit, and the Spirit against the flesh; and these are contrary to one another, so that you do not do the things that you wish" (Galatians 5:17) Peter urges us to "abstain from fleshly lusts which war against the soul" (1 Peter 2:11)

Paul provides us with two rather lengthy lists by which we are able to determine which force within is winning the battle. First of all, he lists various works of the flesh:

- fornication (sexual immorality)

- uncleanness (impurity)

- lasciviousness (debauchery)

- idolatry

127

- sorcery (witchcraft, drugs)

- enmities (hatred)

- strife (discord)

- jealousies

- wraths (fits of rage)

- factions (selfish ambition)

- divisions (dissension)

- parties (heresies)

- envyings

- drunkenness

- revellings (orgies)

- and such like.

He tells them that they that practice such things shall not inherit the kingdom of God. He then lists the fruit of the Spirit:

- love

- joy

- peace

- longsuffering (patience)

- kindness

- goodness

- faithfulness

- meekness (gentleness)

• self-control

The first list leads to destruction; the second leads to life. Who among us does not long for the qualities listed in the second list?

It may very well be the case that you have struggled to obtain the qualities listed as the fruit of the Spirit, but have been unsuccessful. Expect a struggle. Don't be surprised by it. Paul said the struggle would arise because the Spirit and the flesh are contrary to one another. Each one wants the control (Galatians 5:17; Romans 7:17f). But to ensure success in this struggle we must use God's powerful weapons of warfare.

Consider this: the list of favorable qualities is not referred to as the "fruit of Steven Lloyd," but rather the "fruit of the Spirit." "Fruit" here means "result, outcome, deed, product." When we fight against the flesh successfully, the outcome, the fruit thereof, is of God; the Spirit of God. If we have lived with the expectation of acquiring these qualities independent of the Spirit of God, then we have been laboring in vain. No wonder some are worn out and discouraged.

For anyone to enjoy the fruit of the Spirit there are two items that need to be understood. First of all, we need to learn what it means to crucify the flesh. Secondly, we need to learn what it means to walk by the Spirit because Paul said, "Walk by the Spirit, and ye shall not fulfill the lust of the flesh" (5:16).

What does it mean to walk by the Spirit? There are three different phrases used in Galatians 5:16-26 that all mean the same thing:

- walk by the Spirit (5:16)

- led by the Spirit (5:18)

- live by the Spirit (5:25)

These three phrases seem to be equivalent to one another.

- Walk in the Spirit, and you shall not fulfill the lust of the flesh (5:16).

- If you are led by the Spirit, you are not under the law (5:18).

- If we live by the Spirit, let us also walk in the Spirit (5:25).

These texts teach that we are to live according to the instructions of the Spirit of God. These instructions are made known to us in the Word, which all points to our involvement with the Word of God (Ephesians 6:17).

CRUCIFY THE FLESH

After listing the various qualities of the fruit of the Spirit, Paul writes, "And those who are Christ's have crucified the flesh with its passions and desires" (Galatians 5:24). Earlier in this same letter he affirmed this of himself:

> I have been crucified with Christ; it is no longer I who live, but Christ lives in me; and the life which I now live in the flesh I live by faith in the Son of God, who loved me and gave Himself for me (2:20).

When an individual is hanged on a cross, he is put there to die. So the figure of being crucified or having crucified the flesh carries with it the idea of dying.

In Colossians 3:5 Paul said, "Therefore put to death your

members which are on the earth: fornication, uncleanness, passion, evil desire, and covetousness, which is idolatry." When something is put to death it no longer has any power to affect or influence us. Once these things have been put to death they no longer have power over you. We set ourselves up for defeat when we make provisions to fulfill the flesh's desires.

The idea of sin no longer having power over us is masterfully demonstrated in Romans 6. (Please take time now to read Romans 6.) Sin once reigned and had dominion over us and held us in bondage. But notice, in contrast to such bondage, the figure of a death having taken place, a burial and a resurrection in 6:1-6. This is that form of teaching whereby we were delivered out of the bondage of sin—that is, the control sin once had on us.

So what does it mean to crucify the flesh? It means the same thing as:

- putting to death the works of the flesh (sin)
- dying to the works of the flesh
- no longer making provision for the flesh (Rom 13:14)
- no longer walking in these things (that is no longer participating in them)

"And those who are Christ's have crucified the flesh with its passions and desires" (Galatians 5:24).

APPLICATION

Now, if the fruit of the Spirit is not present in your life, it may very well indicate one of two things, or both. You have not yet crucified the flesh (which would include making no provisions for the flesh). Or you are not saturating your mind with the Word of God, letting it control your life. When we surrender ourselves to God, He grants us the power of self-control.

When we fall it is usually due to wrong desires. The only way I know of to alter your desires concerning evil is to meditate on God's Word. One of the Psalmists learned to delight in God's Word, and said:

- I have refrained my feet from every evil way (119:101).

- I hate every false way (119:104).

If you are not yet in Christ, begin by following Paul's instructions in Romans 6. Once in Christ, you must die daily to the passions and the lusts of life. And we must all saturate our minds with the Word of God to ensure lasting results. Then, and only then can it rightly be said that we walk by the Spirit or are led by the Spirit or live by the Spirit. And then we will enjoy the fruit of the Spirit: love, joy, peace, longsuffering, kindness, goodness, faithfulness, meekness, self-control. If any of these are absent from your life, you now know how to incorporate them into your life.

One evening the news featured the story of an elderly Riverside, California man who returned home from the grocery story only to be met by a man lurking behind the bushes at his house. The old man was shot, thrown into a newly dug grave, covered with dirt, and, to top it all off, several planks of wood. The problem was the old man was not dead. He slowly clawed his way through the dirt to the surface, but having lost so much blood he was unable to lift the planks from his partially open grave. He knocked on the wood hoping some passerby would hear him.

Fortunate for him someone did hear him. He was later rushed to the hospital and survived to tell the story.

What is the point? A burial is of little value if the one buried is still alive. Paul affirms of the person who is baptized that they are to be dead to sin. It is only when someone has died to sin that they should be buried. It is only when we have been buried dead that we are raised to walk in newness of life.

Appeal after appeal is made to Romans 6 to affirm the importance of baptism in the conversion process, and rightly so. Paul was reminding the saints in Rome of some very important truths. But the emphasis of the text, at least the first 14 verses, is on death. Read these 14 verses again and circle the word "death," "dead," or any other form of the word. It will surprise you to see the number of times it is used, but it will help you to see what Paul's emphasis in the text is.

ABSTINENCE WORKSHEET

There are obviously many things in this life that are morally neutral that call for moderation. But there are other things in life that are not morally neutral. These are the things from which God calls for us to abstain.

- Beloved, I beg you as sojourners and pilgrims, abstain from fleshly lusts which war against the soul (1 Peter. 2:11).

- But put on the Lord Jesus Christ, and make no provision for the flesh, to fulfill its lusts (Romans 13:14).

Think of how nonsensical the cheer— "Here's to abstinence, as long as it's practiced in moderation"—is in light of such teachings found in Matthew 5:29-30:

And if your right eye causes you to sin, pluck it out and cast it from you; for it is more profitable for you that one of your members perish, than for your whole body to be cast into hell. And if your right hand causes you to sin, cut if off and cast if from you; for it is more profitable for you that one of your members perish, than for your whole body to be cast into hell.

What we all need to learn is how to hate what we love—that we ought to hate. In other words, there may be some aspect of sin we like, but ought to hate. How do I learn to hate it? Much of this goes back to the practice of meditating on God's Word for the renewing of our mind, but more specifically, let me suggest two things. First of all, we need to commit ourselves to walk after the Spirit, and secondly, we need to crucify the flesh.

THINK ABOUT IT

1. Read Galatians 5:16-24

   a. What things does Paul associate with the flesh?

   b. What things listed here trouble you?

   c. List the various characteristics of the fruit of the Spirit.

   d. What other phrases are used that mean the same as walk by the Spirit? (See 5:18, 25).

   e. Fill in the following statements:

   "Walk by the Spirit, and _____" (5:16)

   "If ye are led by the Spirit, _____" (5:18)

   "If we live by the Spirit, _____" (5:25)

   f. All of which means that we are to live according to the instructions and the truth of the Spirit of God. These instructions are made known to us in the Word; which all points to our involvement with the Word of God.

2. Galatians 5:24 reads, "And they that are of Christ Jesus have crucified the flesh with the passions and the lusts thereof."

    a What does it mean to crucify the flesh with the passions and the lusts thereof?

    b Consider these passages:

    - Galatians 2:20

    - Colossians 3:5

    - Romans 6:1-6

    - Romans 13:14

3. If the fruit of the Spirit is not exemplified in your life, it is probably the case that you are not walking by the Spirit, or you have not yet crucified the flesh, or both.

The only way you will ever alter your desire for what is evil is to meditate on God's Word. Because the Psalmist learned to delight in God's Word, he wrote:

- I have restrained my feet from every evil way (Psalm 119:101)

- I hate every false way (Psalm 119:104).

READ & MEDITATE

1. Romans 12:1-2

2. Ephesians 4:17-32

3. Philippians 2:12-13

4. 1 Thessalonians 2:13

12

FELLOWSHIP

Making your way in the world today takes everything you've got. Taking a
break from all your worries would surely help a lot. Wouldn't you like to
get away. Sometimes you want to go where everybody knows your name and
their always glad you came. You want to be where you can see your troubles
are all the same. You want to go where everybody knows your name. —
Theme to Cheers

A number of things occur when we are baptized. Our sins are
washed away (Acts 22:16)—which is the same thing as
saying our sins are remitted or forgiven (Acts 2:38). Another
marvelous thing occurs: the Lord adds us to the church of Christ
(Acts 2:47). Paul put it this way: "For by one Spirit were we all
baptized into the one body" (1 Corinthians 12:13), which is the
church (compare Ephesians 4:4 with Ephesians 1:22-23).

In that one body we experience the sweet blessing of
fellowship. The Psalmist wrote,

Behold, how good and how pleasant it is
For brethren to dwell together in unity!
It is like the precious oil upon the head,
Running down on the beard,
The beard of Aaron,
Running down on the edge of his garments.
It is like the dew of Hermon,
Descending upon the mountains of Zion;
For there the Lord commanded the blessing
Life forevermore (Psalm 133).

King David, reflecting on the blessings of God, has this to say about fellowship with the saints of God: "They are the excellent ones, in whom is all my delight" (Psalm 16:3).

Some people do not find that sweetness due to the fact that they have not yet dealt effectively with past or current problems; and they have not found many open doors to discuss those problems with anyone. This may be the case for a number of reasons. One reason may be that some come to the church and find people who appear to have their act together. Consequently, the newcomer believes there is no one in the church that can relate to him or her, or visa versa. Unfortunately, fellowship is not all it ought to be if that is the case.

It is not uncommon for someone to come to the church wanting to improve his or her quality of life, but to feel intimidated by the scenario I have just described. Ironically, if they had stayed long enough they would have discovered that members of the church do face problems just like everyone else; that they struggle with some of the same issues of life. They would find people who have experienced the same kinds of struggles they have experienced but who have overcome those difficulties. They would have found people who could help them overcome their problems.

Because some Christians think that the church does not deal with their kind of problem they have sought help from support groups outside the fellowship of other Christians. I have asked some of them, "What is it that your support group offers you that you did not find in the church?" They tell me that they found "openness" and someone to talk to who has been where they have been. People are not going to open up unless they think they are in a safe environment.

To protect themselves, people may test a counselor with a hypothetical case. If the counselor passes their test, he is trusted with the real problem. For example, a young woman came to me in tears telling me that a mutual friend of ours was caught up in sexual immorality. She wanted to know what she should do. I told her that the thing to do was not to approve of her friend's behavior, but to encourage her to repent. She wanted to see how I would react to a case distant from hers before she trusted me with the real problem.

I guess I passed her test because months later she trusted me with her problem. She, too, had been caught up in the practice of sexual immorality. I am happy to report that she changed her behavior in her efforts to honor God.

What my friend was looking for was an environment in which she could get help. She knew she was doing wrong. She did not need to be told. I did not need to condemn her. She had already condemned herself. What she needed was help in believing that God had forgiven her. She was looking for an environment where she could be forgiven, understood, and guided. She was looking for security and the power to overcome her sin. Aren't we all!

What better place to seek guidance than God? God will in no wise fail you, neither will He in any wise forsake you (Hebrews 13:5). As for the power to overcome, God is the only provider of such power.

There is only one environment here on earth where security and forgiveness and understanding and guidance can all be found - it's the church. What other organization could you be a part of and enjoy the forgiveness of your sins? or find wise counsel from above? and genuine security? What other organization can help people overcome sin? Oh, they may help you break a bad habit, but they have not taught you how to overcome the penalty for sin. In fact, some of these support groups deny there is such a thing as sin. (A lot of help that would be!)

BENEFITS OF FELLOWSHIP

Consider the benefits that accompany fellowship with the saints of God. First of all, the church provides us with the opportunity to grow through worship and through the preaching of the Word. If the message is biblically sound, and preached in love, those listening with honest and good hearts will grow.

Secondly, there are small groups that meet within the church. If these meetings are centered on the Word of God, and mutual concern for one another, people are afforded the opportunity to discuss their problems, to search the Scriptures for answers, and to pray for one another. Just imagine what great good could come from such meetings.

COPING: A BIBLICAL APPROACH

A third opportunity for growth would be the one-on-one meetings that occur outside a formal worship service and the studies conducted when the church meets. But herein is probably one of the church's greatest weaknesses where fellowship is concerned.

Flavil Yeakley, professor at the University of Tulsa, has studied patterns in the fellowship of the churches of Christ for years. Note these startling findings:

- 10% have no friends in the church

- 30% have friends in the church but do not visit them

- 50% have friends in the church and visit them but there is no spiritual dimension to the visit

- 10% have friends in the church, visit with their friends, and enjoy a spiritual dimension in the visit - but only once a month on the average.

Perhaps these statistics will help us understand why we have not been more effective in helping each other cope with the issues of life.

> For Christians, problems that can be treated by psychological counseling can be better ministered to by biblical counseling within the body of Christ. ——Martin & Deidre Bobgan

Please do not misunderstand me. I am not suggesting that we turn our worship services into support group workshops. It would be a grave mistake indeed to let problems and problem solving set the agenda for what is to be preached. There are many other important things that need to be learned as well. What I am saying is this: we need to demonstrate genuine interest in others

141

and to make ourselves approachable and available to others. I am saying that we need each other. We need the support and encouragement that comes from God and His people.

A LETTER OF EXHORTATION

The writer of the Book of Hebrews leaves his readers with no uncertainty as to the importance of fellowship. The people to whom he wrote were Jews who were being persecuted by other Jews for accepting Jesus as the Christ. The author called it a "great conflict of sufferings" and because of it they were throwing away their confidence. They were:

- coming short of the promised rest (4:1)

- wavering in hope (10:23)

- some had completely fallen away (10:26ff) • shrinking back (10:35)

- beset with the sin of unbelief (12:1)

- fainting in their souls (12:3)

- falling short of the glory of God (12:15)

Throughout the letter there are numerous exhortations, eleven of which begin with the words "Let us..." But the center of gravity for the entire epistle is Hebrews 10:19-25. The author has just completed an elaborate argument (one of the longest sustained arguments in the New Testament) and concludes with this loving exhortation to maintain stedfastness in the face of opposition:

> Therefore, brethren, having boldness to enter the Holiest by the blood of Jesus, by a new and living way which He consecrated for us, through

the veil, that is, His flesh, and having a High Priest over the house of God, let us draw near with a true heart in full assurance of faith, having our hearts sprinkled from an evil conscience and our bodies washed with pure water. Let us hold fast the confession of our hope without wavering, for He who promised is faithful. And let us consider one another in order to stir up love and good works, not forsaking the assembling of ourselves together, as is the manner of some, but exhorting one another, and so much the more as you see the Day approaching (Hebrews 10:19-25).

This text identifies some of the reasons why we should not forsake the fellowship of the saints. It confirms the fact that we need the encouragement that comes from God and each other.

First of all, we cannot draw near to God by forsaking the assembling of ourselves together. The expression "draw near" is used characteristically with reference to our worship before God. How then can we "draw near" without "drawing near?" We are to draw near in fullness of faith. This is especially significant when you realize that the besetting sin of the Hebrews was that of unbelief; and without fullness of faith it is impossible to be well pleasing to God (Hebrews 12:1; 11:6). In 10:35ff, the reader is exhorted, "Therefore do not cast away your confidence, which has great reward. For you have need of endurance, so that after you have done the will of God, you may receive the promise." Hebrews 11 contains numerous examples of people who drew near to God in fullness of faith. So, we should faithfully assemble ourselves together in order to draw near to God.

Second, we should not forsake the assembling of ourselves together, that the confession of our hope waver not: "...having our hearts sprinkled from an evil conscience and our bodies washed with pure water. Let us hold fast the confession of our hope without wavering" (10:22-23). The people to whom this letter was written were an embattled people. They had need of great encouragement to keep on keeping on; an encouragement they would miss by forsaking the assembling of themselves together. Without faith there can be no hope. Without hope there is no incentive to remain faithful. This same writer says, "Let us hold fast the confession of our hope" in contrast with casting away their boldness (10:35). We should faithfully assemble ourselves together with the saints that the confession of our hope waver not.

Third, we should faithfully assemble ourselves together to consider one another to provoke (stir up) unto love and good works. Considering again the statistics Flavil Yeakley provides us ought to bolster the fact that assembling ourselves together and encouragement go hand in hand. When we meet we are to stir one another up to love and good works. Can this be done when absent? In the closing chapter of this epistle there are five exhortations strung together:

- Let brotherly love continue (13:1)
- Do not forget to entertain strangers (13:2)
- Remember the prisoners as if chained with them (13:3)
- Marriage is honorable among all, and the bed undefiled (13:4)
- Let your conduct be without covetousness (13:5)

Note how genuine love is at the root of each of these exhortations.

Another reason we are to stir one another up to love and good works is expressed by Paul: "For we are his workmanship, created in Christ Jesus for good works, which God afore prepared that we should walk in them" (Ephesians 2:10).

The reason for this particular exhortation is that neglecting the assembly would in time lead to the desertion of the faith and a wavering of hope. There is a direct correlation between assembling together and faithfulness. This is not to say that everyone who attends every service is faithful; and it is not to say that if someone misses a service for some legitimate reason he is not faithful. But the strength of our faith and the stedfastness of our hope are dependent upon the encouragement we give and get from one another. The maintenance of love and good works is dependent on the same. How can we hope to consider one another to provoke to love and good works while forsaking the assembling of ourselves together?

Another reason given in the text is "the day drawing nigh." What is or was the day drawing nigh? To cut through all of the possibilities, I believe this reference points to the destruction of Jerusalem in 70 A.D for the following reasons. First of all, the temple was a part of the first covenant.

> The destruction of Jerusalem and the temple would be of signal importance to those Hebrew Christians who were clinging to that old system or were tempted; to leave Christ and return to it…That was one of the main problems described in the epistle…Such a fearful day of impending judgment would remind the readers of the dangers of neglect and apostasy. —John Waddey

The destruction of the temple and of Jerusalem in 70 A.D.

was a judgment of God. It was an awful day, with countless men and women being murdered. But in application, the day of God's judgment will one day be upon us. With that in mind, we should exhort one another unto love and good works as we contemplate the coming of the last day—the Judgment day.

This text is designed to exhort brethren to "fullness of faith," and to an "unwavering hope," and to "love and good works."

I hope that each of us will have the eyes to see the need we all have for the encouragement that comes from God and others. I hope we will all see how important fellowship is.

FELLOWSHIP WORKSHEET

People who are uninformed of the basic principles of Christianity often ask the question, "Do I have to go to church to go to heaven?" As kindly as I know how, I tell them that for the Christian the emphasis is not on their obligation to attend, but rather the great need to come together. The one who loves God is compelled by that love to express their adoration to God for all the favors He bestows on their life. But there is another dimension to fellowship that I would like for us to focus on in this chapter.

THINK ABOUT IT

1. What ideals come to mind when you think of the word "fellowship?"

2. What purposes do you see fellowship fulfilling? (READ Hebrews 10:19-26)

3. What is the basis for fellowship?

    a. 1 Corinthians 1:10

    b. 1 John 1:1-10

    c. 1 John 4:7-21

    d. Ephesians 4:1-6

4. The saints of the first century met daily (Acts 2:46, 27). a. Why do you suppose they met so often?

    b. Did they need more in the way of fellowship than we do today?

5. Why don't Christians go to other Christians with problems that are spiritual in nature? Why do some trust those outside the fellowship of Christ with the same?

READ AND MEDITATE

1. Psalm 133

STEVEN M. LLOYD

13

REMAINING CURRENT

Let not the sun go down upon thy wrath; neither give place to the devil. —
Paul

L et me explain what I mean by remaining current. If a conflict
arises and it is not remedied as soon as possible, ground is
being given for that conflict to escalate.

For example, the apostle Paul spoke of a particular conflict
two men, Hymenaeus and Philetus, had with the word of God
concerning the resurrection. These men said the resurrection had
already passed, thus overthrowing the faith of some. Paul
compares their words with gangrene (2 Timothy 2:16-17).
Gangrene, by definition, refers to dead and decaying tissue in
some part of the body due to the failure of an adequate blood
supply to the decaying tissue. If not halted, the infected portions
of the body would need to be amputated. Errors like the one Paul
was addressing can spread like gangrene if we are not careful to

149

treat them immediately.

In his Galatian letter, Paul tells of some who were sneaking into the church for no other purpose than to cause trouble. These troublers were seeking to pervert the truth of the Gospel. Writing with reference to the conflict, Paul said, "…we did not yield submission even for an hour, that the truth of the gospel might continue with you" (Galatians 2:5).

In the very next paragraph, Paul tells us about a conflict he had with the apostle Peter. Peter's actions threatened the truth of the gospel also.

> …for before certain men came from James, he would eat with the Gentiles; but when they came, he withdrew and separated himself, fearing those who were of the circumcision. And the rest of the Jews also played the hypocrite with him, so that even Barnabas was carried away with their hypocrisy (Galatians 2:12-13).

Paul began this paragraph by saying, "when Peter had come to Antioch, I withstood him to his face, because he was to be blamed" (Galatians 2:11).

In teaching us how to walk worthily of our calling, Paul writes: "Be angry, and do not sin: do not let the sun go down on your wrath nor give place to the devil" (Ephesians 4:26-27).

These passages are examples of conflicts being addressed on the spot. Just imagine the potential trouble these problems could have caused if they had not been dealt with immediately.

Now consider how some of your own conflicts grew to incredible proportions because you did not deal with them as they arose. Imagine the eternal consequences that await those who say

"I'll deal with my sin tomorrow" when "Today" is the day of salvation (Hebrews 3:13-15).

A counselor I used to listen to on the radio compared conflicts to earthquakes. Just as earthquakes have epicenters and aftershocks, so problems have their epicenters and aftershocks. We could say that the epicenter of a problem is the time the problem occurred. Aftershocks would be like the consequences that arise from not having dealt with the problem at the time it occurred.

Using the metaphor of the earthquake, I can even imagine there being numerous epicenters in a person's life with a host of aftershocks. If problems are not resolved at the time they occur, can you imagine not being able to discern what aftershock belongs to what earthquake? Or whether we are experiencing an earthquake or aftershock?

I know a man who confessed to telling so many lies in his life, that, pausing in the middle of a story he was telling, he embarrassingly admitted that he could not remember if the story he was telling us was a lie or the truth. It reminds me of something my grandfather used to say: "Son, if you tell one lie, you'll have to tell a thousand others to cover up the initial one." Life can become rather confusing.

We can eliminate a lot of unnecessary trouble from our lives if we learn to remain current with the problems we face; if we effectively address the problems as they arise.

Let's take a look at how to stay on top of things.

SECRET SIN

Secret sin is sin that an individual commits, but in secret. No one knows about it but him (and God). Perhaps he has nurtured unlawful thoughts and ideas about someone who is not his own, as in a man lusting after a woman. The problem may include jealousy and envy. Because he does not act on it, it remains secret; nevertheless it is a work of the flesh (Galatians 5:20).

Paul wrote, "Some men's sins are evident, going before unto judgment; and some men also they follow after" (1 Timothy 5:24). He also wrote, "God will judge the secrets of men" according to the gospel, by Jesus Christ (Romans 2:16). God can do so because He knows the hearts of men. "For the Lord does not see as man sees; for man looks at the outward appearance, but the Lord looks at the heart" (1 Samuel 16:7). To the Pharisees, Jesus said, "You are those who justify yourselves before men, but God knows your hearts" (Luke 16:15).

How should we deal with secret sin? First of all, let me say that it should not be viewed lightly simply because others are not aware of it. Even though we may have been able to hide our dark deeds from the eyes of the world, "…there is no creature hidden from His sight, but all things are naked and open to the eyes of Him to whom we must give account" (Hebrews 4:13).

As Christians we are to repent, that is, have a change of mind concerning what we have done, and ask God to forgive us. As one man said, "The best place for the brethren to get right with the Lord is in their own closet."

Remember what Jesus said concerning this:

But you, when you pray, go into your room, and when you have shut your door, pray to your Father who is in the secret place; and your Father who sees in secret will reward you openly" (Matthew 6:6).

And John wrote:

If we confess our sins, He is faithful and just to forgive us our sins and to cleanse us from all unrighteousness (1 John 1:9). and the blood of Jesus Christ His Son cleanses us from all sin (1 John 1:7).

BROTHER AGAINST BROTHER

Moreover if your brother sins against you, go and tell him his fault between you and him alone. If he hears you, you have gained your brother. But if he will not hear you, take with you one or two more, that by the mouth of two or three witnesses every word may be established. And if he refuses to hear them, tell it to the church. But if he refuses even to hear the church, let him be to you like a heathen and a tax collector (Matthew 18:15-17).

It is not uncommon for someone to tell me that someone else has sinned against them. My first question is, "Is this something I need to be hearing?" I then remind them of Jesus' teachings in Matthew 18:15-17.

- First go to the brother and show him his fault "between you and him alone"

- If he refuse to hear you, take with you one or two more "that by the mouth of two or three witnesses every word may be established."

- If that doesn't work, then tell it to the church and have no company with him. If handling a conflict on a private basis doesn't work, then it must become public.

- If the erring brother responds properly, "you have gained your brother."

There was a student at the Bible school I attended who would leave the room every ten minutes during a test, then come back and answer a question on the exam. Another student observed him doing this and began to stew inside thinking the other student was cheating. When he asked me what he should do I suggested he approach the "erring" student. By the way, this was not the first time this kind of behavior during a test had been observed. The student who observed his "erring" classmate suspiciously leave the room was reluctant to approach his classmate, but did, and found out that the "erring" student had a kidney condition which caused him to make frequent visits to the restroom.

Brother Curious told me that he was reluctant to question the student concerning his conduct but was glad he did and that it proved to him the wisdom of our Lord (Matthew 18). The student in question also thanked the other student for coming to him and asking him about his behavior rather than harboring bad thoughts about him.

PUBLIC SIN

What about open public sin – sin that is not secret, but is known or has the potential of being made known to the church and the community?

The nature of this kind of sin is not to be compared with a brother sinning against another brother in a private way. It may be safe to say that at the onset, sin must be rebuked and dealt with in as open a way as the sin itself.

It is not always necessary to first approach a person privately. For example, Paul wrote an open letter to Corinth rebuking the young man who had his father's wife. He also rebuked the church for being so "open-minded" about the whole affair (1 Corinthians 5).

When Peter challenged the truth of the gospel by his hypocritical and prejudicial behavior in Antioch, Paul "withstood him to his face, because he was to be blamed" (Galatians 2:11) He rebuked Peter "before them all" (Galatians 2:14).

The difference between the second and third situation is the extent to which the sin is known and the extent to which it affected others. When sin has been committed by one brother against another brother, the matter must be dealt with, first of all, on a private basis. If that does not work, then it needs to be made public. When one man's sin affects so many others, as in Peter's case, it must be dealt with publicly so that all concerned may be warned and instructed.

My instructor in ministerial counseling, Hugh Shira, used to illustrate the difference in this way. Let us say that in math class a student makes an error on paper while at his seat. All the teacher needs to do, as he or she roams the class, is stop at the desk of the student in error and help him to correct his mistake. But if that same student had been in front of the entire class at the chalk board and made an error in his figuring, then the teacher would be obligated to correct the mistake in front of the entire class because the entire class would have been exposed to the mistake.

Once a person has been confronted with their sin, they must repent and confess that sin. When Simon asked to buy the power of the Holy Spirit he was told, "Repent therefore of this your wickedness, and pray God if perhaps the thought of your heart may be forgiven you" (Acts 8:22). James instructs us to "Confess your trespasses to one another, and pray for one another…" (James 5:16) Notice we are to confess our sins one to another. I do not know what good it does to simply come before the church to say we have not been living right or have not been as faithful as we should be. Sin should be confessed. And until a person is willing to confess their sin they should not respond.

Why are we so hesitant to confess our sins to one another? Some are afraid of gossip. But think with me for a moment: The confession of sin should stop the gossip. If we came forward saying we have sinned but did not specify what it was, this turns on the gossip switch. People begin to speculate. But what happens when the sin itself is confessed? It leaves no room for speculation, and stops the gossip because there is nothing left to be said. At this point brethren help brethren rebuild their lives and pray for one another.

SINS COMMITTED BY THE MAN IN THE WORLD
God loves all men and wants all men to be saved:

- For God so loved the world that He gave His only begotten Son, that whoever believes in Him should not perish but have everlasting life (John 3:16).

- But God demonstrates His own love toward us, in that while we were still sinners, Christ died for us (Romans 5:8).

- (God) desires all men to be saved, and to come to the knowledge of the truth (1 Timothy 2:4).

- (God is) not willing that any should perish but that all should come to repentance (2 Peter 3:9).

Unfortunately, we have all subjected ourselves to the wrath of God due to sin (Romans. 1:18). But God has not left us without a means for gaining pardon from sin. By the goodness of God, men are led to repentance (Romans. 2:4). All throughout the Book of Acts, we find the following pattern. When the gospel reached the ears of the lost, they were encouraged to believe in God and to believe that He raised Jesus Christ from the dead, declaring him to be the Son of God (Romans 1:4). Based on that belief, they were exhorted to repent, to confess their faith in Jesus of Nazareth as the Son of God, and to be baptized for the forgiveness of their sins (Mark 16:16; Acts 2:28; Acts 22:16; Romans 6:1-6; Galatians 3:26).

The one who is in Christ enjoys every spiritual blessing (Ephesians 1:3), which includes the cleansing blood of Christ, as he is walking in the light. Should he err, he must repent, confess, and pray.

When the gospel was preached to the apostle Paul, Ananias, the preacher on that occasion, said to him "And now why are you waiting?" (Acts 22:16). When Paul preached the gospel to his jailor in Philippi, we are told that he was baptized "the same hour of the night...immediately" (Acts 16:33). What time was that? Sometime after midnight (16:25).

Why the urgency in remaining current with our problems? Because leaving them to fester on their own, we reap the consequences we least desire. I know from experience that addressing a conflict is not a pleasant thing to do. Sometimes it is the last thing I want to do, but I have learned through experience that if I do not deal with the problems as they arise, the fretting and anxiety I find myself living with, in the meantime, is far worse than dealing with the problem in its infancy stage.

REMAINING CURRENT WORKSHEET

Many of us foolishly avoid confronting the problems of life, thinking they will just go away. Some actually ignore them by pretending they do not exist. Others refuse to address the issues they repeatedly face, claiming that they have put them all on the back burner until they settle a problem they had years ago. Many times this is nothing more than an excuse not to deal with anything at all. Oh, what a mess this can make of life. Disaster lurks at every turn if this is the strategy we have adopted in coping with life's challenges.

THINK ABOUT IT

1. Why do we put off until tomorrow what we could address today?

2. Why are we so reluctant to approach one another concerning matters of offense?

   a. pride

   b. misplaced priorities

   c. ignorance

   d. fear of:

      i. rejection

      ii. anger

    iii. being misunderstood

  e. we do not think our feelings are valid

3. How is remaining current related to fellowship? (2 Corinthians 6:14ff)

4. How ought we to deal with the following scenarios:

  a. secret sin

  b. brother against brother

  c. public sin

  d. a sinner outside of Christ

5. Do any of the preceding describe a situation in which you find yourself? How ought you to handle it?

All of us have needs. When those needs are not met, and we do not confront the issue at hand, it can quickly arouse our anger. If our anger is not confronted, bitterness is right around the corner. Perhaps you have let some problem escalate to the extent of bitterness. What is God's remedy for bitterness? See Ephesians 4:31-32 and Colossians 3:12-15.

READ AND MEDITATE

1. Matthew 5:21-26

2. Romans 12:17-21

STEVEN M. LLOYD

14

LONELINESS

I will never leave you nor forsake you. —The Lord

I know of no better description of loneliness than the one provided by Solomon in Ecclesiastes:

There is one alone, without companion:

> He has neither son nor brother.
> Yet there is no end to all his labors,
> Nor is his eye satisfied with riches.
> But he never asks,
> "For whom do I toil and deprive myself of good?"
> This also is vanity and a grave misfortune.
>
> Two are better than one,
> Because they have a good reward for their labor.
> For if they fall, one will lift up his companion.
> But woe to him who is alone when he falls,
> For he has no one to help him up.
> Again, if two lie down together, they will keep warm;

But how can one be warm alone?

Though one may be overpowered by another, two can withstand him.

And a threefold cord is not quickly broken (Ecclesiastes 4:8-12).

What is significant about this particular picture of loneliness is that it describes someone who is alone "under the sun." This expression finds its way into Ecclesiastes twenty-eight times, and for good reason. The "under the sun" perspective on life is what life looks like without God. It is a description of the way things appear "under the sun" as opposed to life being seen from the above the sun perspective; life as seen by God and with God.

With God in the picture one may be alone, but not lonely. Take the apostle Paul for example. While he was awaiting his execution, he wrote to Timothy: "At my first defense no one stood with me, but all forsook me. May it not be charged against them. But the Lord stood with me and strengthened me" (2 Timothy 4:16,17).

The Christian never needs to feel totally abandoned. If we are what we ought to be toward one another, we will love each other at all times (Proverbs 17:17). And the Lord Himself will not abandon us. He says, "I will never leave you nor forsake you" (Hebrews 13:5). This being the case, we can say, "The Lord is my helper; I will not fear" (Hebrews 13:6; Psalm 118:6).

God's faithfulness is a manifestation of His genuine love. To understand and believe in the love of God are two crucial elements to any person's effectiveness in coping with sin and other issues in life.

LONELINESS

Loneliness can be devastating. For example, one of my favorite authors describes the loneliest point of life in these terms:

> My despondency derived from the loneliness of living alone without any
> emotional attachments and from what I felt was the withering of my
> intellectual resources. I drew no satisfaction from past achievements—
> books written, work done. The future could not have looked blanker or
> bleaker" (Adler 1977, p. 319).

In his despondency, the author made two lists: one list of his
assets and one list of his liabilities. Under the latter, he included a
two-year vacation from his normal work routines, lack of drive,
lack of clear objectives, all of which pointed, in his mind, to
quitting his university work, getting out of academic life, and
possible suicide. Mr. Adler viewed himself as unable to establish a
good relationship with his two adopted sons. And he had inflicted
his marriage with irreparable damage by carrying on an "affair."

His loneliness was produced by alienating himself from his
family by unacceptable behavior. His loneliness stemmed from
"living alone without any emotional attachment" and from what
he felt was "the withering of his intellectual resources." (Even
intellectual pursuits provide no lasting meaning when divorced
from God (See Proverbs 1:7). This is quite a loss when you
consider the fact that Mr. Adler had been the editor-in-chief of
the Encyclopedia Britannica and of the Great Books of the
Western World for decades.

Remember Solomon's description of the lonely man? There is
one alone, without companion:

- he has neither son nor brother
- he deprives himself, but for whom?

163

- there is no one to help him in his work

- there is no one to lift him when he falls

- there is no one to help keep him warm when it is cold

- there is no one to help him ward off evildoers.

It is no wonder that some despair even of life itself under these conditions. Mosie Lister acknowledges the despair that accompanies being alone in the song "Where No One Stands Alone."

Once I stood in the night with my head bowed low,
 In the darkness as black as could be;
And my heart felt alone and I cried, O Lord,
Don't hide Your face from me.

Like a king I may live in a palace so tall,
With great riches to call my own;
But I don't know a thing in this whole wide world
That's worse than being alone.

And in the chorus there is a cry to God for comfort:

Hold my hand all the way,
Every hour, every day,
From here to the great unknown.
Take my hand; Let me stand
Where no one stands alone.

THE CAUSE OF LONELINESS

I recall hearing a radio counselor talking to a young man about his loneliness. The counselor asked the young man a peculiar question. Concerning the caller's loneliness he asked, "Who's missing?" That question got me to thinking. Is it possible for someone to be surrounded by family and friends and still feel alone? Is it possible for a person to be without anyone around, say, to live alone, and not feel lonely?

After making us all think, the radio host finally made his point. If we are lonely, it is most likely the case that we are missing. We may have trouble living with what we have done or with what we have become, so we avoid keeping company with ourselves. We can hardly stand to live with ourselves. And the only way we can avoid company with ourselves is to lose touch with ourselves.

The only remedy I know of to alleviate such an unenviable condition is to follow the principles outlined thus far in this book. Let's look at Mr. Adler again for our example. One of the critical elements missing from his life when he despaired of life itself was a clear objective in life. He had no purpose for living. He drew no satisfaction from past achievements. But, choosing to magnify God in one's life can help bring purpose back into that life. And in so doing, God brings genuine satisfaction into our lives (Ecclesiastes 3:13).

Mr. Adler brought on much of his own despondency as a result of his "affair." Although he does not elaborate on the details of this affair, admittedly, it did irreparable damage to his home life. The problem was sin.

Who was missing in Mr. Adler's life when he was lonely? He had several faithful friends who stood by him. He even took full responsibility for his actions and their consequences. I submit to you that Mr. Adler did not care to be with himself. And when a person gets to that point in his life, I do not care how full the house is, loneliness is bound to follow.

Of course, there is a sense in which we all grow lonely if we live alone and have little to no contact with others. That is what the church is for; to give us what we need in the way of companionship and friendship. I contend that the Christian never needs to be lonely, even if alone.

LONELINESS AND FEAR

Fear often sets in when a person feels alone. This being the case, the Scriptures are replete with exhortations from God encouraging us not to fear.

What I want to demonstrate here is that there is a correlation between fear and unbelief. The greater one's faith, the more fearless he will be. The less one's faith, the more fearful he will be. First of all, let's survey some of the passages that connect fear and faith.

- Be strong and of good courage, do not fear nor be afraid of them; for the Lord your God, He is the One who goes with you. He will not leave you nor forsake you (Deuteronomy 31:6).

- Have I not commanded you? Be strong and of good courage; do not be afraid, nor be dismayed, for the Lord your God is with you wherever you go (Joshua 1:9).

- Do not be afraid of their faces, For I am with you to deliver you, says the Lord (Read all of Jeremiah 1:4-10).

- After commissioning His disciples Jesus said, "Lo, I am with you always, even to the end of the age" (Matthew 28:20).

- But even if you should suffer for righteousness' sake, you are blessed. And do not be afraid of their threats, nor be troubled. But sanctify the Lord God in your hearts, and always be ready to give a defense to everyone who asks you a reason for the hope that is in you, with meekness and fear; (1 Peter 3:14,15).

Throughout the Scriptures we are told not to fear. But we are told to fear God. Solomon said, "Fear God and keep his commandments" (Ecclesiastes 12:13). Peter wrote, "Honor all people. Love the brotherhood. Fear God. Honor the king" (1 Peter 2:17). Of course, slavish fear is not to characterize the Christian. Paul said that we were not saved to live in the spirit of bondage again unto fear, but that we "received the Spirit of adoption by whom we cry out, Abba, Father" (Romans 8:15). John tells us that perfect love casts out fear of judgment (1 John 4:18). We are to:

- perfect holiness in the fear of God (2 Corinthians 7:1)

- subject ourselves one to another in the fear of Christ (Ephesians 5:20)

- work out our own salvation with fear and trembling (Philippians 2:12)

- pass the time of our sojourning in fear (1 Peter 1:17)

- be ready to give answer to every man that asks us a reason concerning our hope, yet with meekness and fear (1 Peter 3:15)

Here is the key point. When one fears God in the way described by the writers of Scripture, one need fear nothing else because God is with him! When a man lives with the knowledge and faith that God is with him, he will fear no evil. He can say with David, "Yea, though I walk through the valley of the shadow of death, I will fear no evil" (Psalm 23:4). And with good courage we may say, "The Lord is my helper; I will not fear: What can man do to me?" (Hebrews 13:6 quoting Psalm 118:6). God said, "But whoever listens to me will dwell safely, and will be secure, without fear of evil" (Proverbs 1:33). Consider the list of blessings in a Psalm that has for its theme fearing God:

> He will not be afraid of evil tidings;
> His heart is steadfast, trusting in the Lord.
> His heart is established; He will not be afraid, Until he sees his desire upon his enemies (Psalm 112:7-8).

But notice what happens when men fear someone or something other than God.

> The children of Ephraim, being armed and carrying bows, turned back in the day of battle.
> They did not keep the covenant of God;
> They refused to walk in His law,
> And forgot His works And His wonders that He had shown them (Psalm 78:9-11).

Fear God and there should be no need to fear anything else.

THE SHADOW OF DEATH

The poet-king, David, boldly said "Yea, though I walk through the valley of the shadow of death, I will fear no evil;" (Psalm 23:4). The American Standard Version footnotes the phrase "shadow of death" and suggests that it literally means "deep darkness (and so elsewhere)." The New English Bible translates it "dark as death." Others have suggested the wording "very deep shadow" and "total darkness." It is a phrase that occurs nearly twenty times in the Old Testament; nine times in the Book of Job; four times in the Psalms; and four times in three prophets.

Job equates it with "a land dark as midnight" and a place where there is no order (10:21,22). God asked Job, "Have the gates of death been revealed unto thee? Or hast thou seen the gates of the shadow of death?" (38:17). Here "the gates of death" are paralleled with the phrase "the gates of the shadow of death." So, the shadow of death is equated with death itself in this passage.

Jeremiah describes the desert as "a land that no one crossed and where no one dwelt" and as "the shadow of death" (Jeremiah 2:6). He exhorts the people of his day to give glory to God before He "turns the light into the shadow of death and makes it gross darkness" (13:16).

One of the Psalmists equates the shadow of death with being bound in affliction and iron, and deliverance from such oppression as being rescued from "the shadow of death" (Ps. 107: 10, 14).

Each writer that uses this phrase employs it metaphorically. When David spoke of the shadow of death he paints for us a valley of danger and deep darkness through which the shepherd leads his sheep. While the most obvious allusion is of impending death, or the threat of death, it is not restricted to death alone.

> If the literal picture is a dark, dangerous valley through which fearful sheep must be led, what are the human applications? What are the dark valleys through which God leads us? Centuries of Christian experience, as well as most English translations, have fixed the meaning particularly on one answer, namely, death. There is, however, no good reason to limit the human meanings to just one. The dark valleys of our lives in the world include adversity, loneliness, depression, temptation or sin.—Leland Ryken.

What is the valley of the shadow of death? Anywhere the threat of death, or loneliness, or depression, temptation, or sin is found. We have all been there! But how did we fare? How well did we cope under it's shadow?

Remember what David said, "Yea, though I walk through the

valley of the shadow of death, I will fear no evil." Why would he fear no evil? "For You are with me. Your rod and Your staff, they comfort me." David is saying that he will not fear the dark valleys of adversity, loneliness, depression, temptation, or sin because Jehovah is His shepherd. David knew and trusted in the fact that God would in no wise fail him, nor in anywise forsake him.

> What have I to dread, what have I to fear
> Leaning on the everlasting arms;
> I have blessed peace with my Lord so near,
> Leaning on the everlasting arms.
> Leaning, Leaning, Safe and secure from all alarms;
> Leaning, Leaning, Leaning on the everlasting arms.

LONELINESS WORKSHEET

Loneliness and aloneness are very close in meaning, but they are not identical. A person may live alone and yet not be lonely because they have friends to visit and family to care for them. But loneliness that is brought on by alienating ourselves from others due to sin can not only make us lonely, it can result in aloneness.

THINK ABOUT IT

1. Read Ecclesiastes 4:8-12

   a. Why does this depict not only someone who is alone, but someone who is also lonely?

   b. What would make a difference for this person? (Remember to consider the context of the Book of Ecclesiastes as a whole.)

2. What scenario best describes your situation?

a. live alone, but not lonely

b. live alone, and lonely

c. lonely

d. The Lord strengthens you

- Why, do you suppose, you are in the condition you chose from the list above?

- Has sin, in any way, alienated you from others? How?

3. How would you have responded to the radio counselor if he had asked you the question, "If you are lonely, who's missing?"

4. What must you do to address the issue of sin in order to alleviate the alienation you feel from God and others? (You may want to refer back to the preceding chapter on remaining current.)

5. What relationship exists between loneliness and fear

6. Review the section titled "The Shadow of Death" in this chapter and describe it in your own words describe.

a. Does the shadow of death relate to what you may be experiencing? If so, how?

b. What would it take to get you to say with David, "Yea, though I walk through the shadow of death, I will fear no evil?"

7. What did the writer, E. A. Hoffman, mean when he spoke of "leaning on the everlasting arms, safe and secure from all alarm"?

READ AND MEDITATE

1. Deuteronomy 31:6

2. Joshua 1:9

3. Psalm 23

4. Jeremiah 1:4-10

15

VALUE

I see no reason for attributing to man a significance different in kind from that which belongs to a baboon or a grain of sand. —Oliver Wendell Holmes

Adversity has shipwrecked the faith of many. In fact, the greatest weapon in the atheist's arsenal is this old argument: God cannot be infinite in goodness and at the same time infinite in power, because such a Being would eliminate sin and suffering insofar as is possible. No one can effectively deny that sin and suffering exists. Therefore, it is argued, the God of the Bible cannot exist. If there is a God, He must be deficient either in goodness or in power. In part, the error in this line of thinking is that no meaning or value is ever attached to the suffering we may experience.

God's existence provides us with the very reason we are able to attach any meaning or value to the problems we face. If God does not exist, the trials we face could never be related to any ultimate meaning or value.

> Real Human Problems are trivialized by reducing them to
> pathologies, thus robbing our everyday struggles of any dignity or
> meaning. —William Kilpatrick

The psychological society has reduced our trouble to pathologies. Pathology is a "scientific study of the nature of diseases, its causes, processes, developments and consequences" (American Heritage Dictionary p. 960). Consequently, our problems are no longer viewed as spiritual, but rather as diseases.

According to the brother of our Lord, trials and temptations serve a purpose; that purpose being to prove or test our faith. He writes,

> My brethren, count it all joy when you fall into various trials, knowing
> that the testing of your faith produces patience. But let patience have its
> perfect work, that you may be perfect and complete, lacking nothing
> (James 1:2-4).

Why were they to count it a joy when tested by various kinds of trials? Because these trials are "the testing of your faith," and the testing of one's faith produces endurance. The only way we can learn to overcome or endure is to have our faith tested by the various trials in life.

James went on to say that we should let this process run its course. In other words, do not try to resist the test. Let it run its course so that you may benefit from it; so that you may become complete and entire, lacking in nothing.

> Christianity challenges men to think on the most serious and far-
> reaching questions which can confront man. These are questions
> which confront every man who thinks deeply at any time in his life.

> The questions are: What is man? Who is God like? What is the origin, the duty, and the destiny of man? How ought I to treat my fellowmen? Does life have meaning? To what cause or causes should I devote my time, ability, and possessions? Christ calls on men to think on life's meaning and to live meaningful lives. —James D. Bales

BENEFITS

Let's take a look at some of the benefits that can come from the trials of life. First of all, the trials we face can reveal where our loyalties lie. Abraham was told to offer Isaac, his son according to promise, as a sacrifice to God. Isaac was the one through whom God vowed to fulfill His promise that in Abraham's seed all the families of the earth would be blessed (Genesis 21:12). Abraham knew that if Isaac were to be sacrificed God would of necessity need to raise him from the dead in order to fulfill His promise.

> By faith Abraham, when he was tested, offered up Isaac, and he who had received the promises offered up his only begotten son, of whom it was said, "In Isaac your seed shall be called," accounting that God was able to raise him up, even from the dead, from which he also received him in a figurative sense (Hebrews 11:17-19).

How familiar are you with the promises God has given to men today? And how much do you trust in them and live your life counting on them?

Another benefit derived from the trials of life is the character that is developed. The saints of the first century were an embattled class of people who suffered many things for their faith. Paul argues that the things they suffered produced character. He writes,

> And we rejoice in the hope of the glory of God. Not only so, but we also

175

rejoice in our sufferings, because we know that suffering produces perseverance; perseverance, character; and character, hope" (NIV Romans 5:2b-4).

Trials afford us the opportunity to place things in their proper perspective. For example, when Paul wrote to the saints at Corinth he described the difficulties he suffered as an apostle in these terms: "We are hard pressed on every side...we are perplexed ...persecuted...struck down...always carrying about in the body the dying of the Lord Jesus...For we who live are always delivered to death for Jesus' sake" (2 Corinthians 4:8-11). Later in this same chapter he referred to this string of downhearted clauses as light and momentary affliction (4:17).

How is it possible to view such a downtrodden existence as light and momentary afflictions? ANSWER: only when it is compared to something heavier and longer lasting. Paul was comparing these difficulties in life to a far more exceeding and eternal weight of glory (4:17). He sent the same message to the saints in Rome: "For I consider that the sufferings of this present time are not worthy to be compared with the glory that shall be revealed in us" (Romans 8:18).

Trials can also alert us to how dependent we are on God. When we are stripped of family and friends and possessions and health, what else, or who else, is there to turn for help? Of course, many trials have the potential for becoming a means of despair, perhaps even our eventual demise, but they can also become a springboard to spiritual growth.

> Every difficulty, and seeming injustice in life has healthful meaning beyond itself, and each drawback has a good answer in Christianity.

The religion Christ left on earth helps one to cope with it all, even the final 'injustice' -- death. So, with courage, we may endure. With confidence, we may fully live. With hope, we may beam with contented determination. Busy with all that, we will stumble into Heaven before we know it. —Jerry Moffitt

When we learn to face the trials of life with joy rather than dread, I am persuaded that we will disarm those trials of their lethal potential to otherwise devastate us. We will keep these problems from becoming even bigger than they need be.

PHILOSOPHY OF DESPAIR

The reality of death, that man is mortal, seems to be the greatest injustice in life. Being such, it has provoked men to search for meaning to life. Many philosophers have tied the reality of death to the very meaning of life: "Since there is death, what meaning does my life have?" William Barrett has commented:

This question is reached naturally as a result of facing the truth about how we really stand in relation to death, a truth which is at odds with the way people normally think and talk about ideas (Barrett p. 82).

The question of meaning is the fundamental question that every man puts to himself. In fact, the question has a direct relationship to God.

More consequences for thought and action follow from the affirmation or denial of God than from answering any other basic question. —Mortimer Adler

If there is a God, and if He has revealed Himself to man through the Bible, I would be wise to learn all I can about Him and how I can please Him. Even the founder and former director of the Goddard Institute for Space and Science Research

177

recognizes this fact. Dr. Robert Jastrow, well-known science writer and agnostic, argues that if there is a God "then He is not only our Creator, but also our sovereign, and we should inform ourselves about the conduct He desires, both with reference to Himself and to our fellow man."

If there is no God and no afterlife, then there will be no final judgment concerning our conduct in this life. Paul argues this case in 1 Corinthians 15. He is addressing those who claim that the dead are not raised. If there is no resurrection from the dead, then there is no survival of the soul after death. Paul says if the dead are not raised:

- Why are some baptized for the dead? (15:29)

- Why do we stand in jeopardy every hour? (15:30)

- Why did he fight wild beasts at Ephesus? (15:32)

And then he says, "If the dead do not rise, let us eat and drink, for tomorrow we die" (15:32). He then warns them that evil companions corrupt good morals. If there is no resurrection of the dead, or if there is no life after death, what is there to restrain us from evil conduct?

One of the more predominant philosophies of the modern world is called existentialism. It is void of answers to the question of meaning. It is a philosophy that fills the human heart with anxiety. In fact, a book was published several decades ago titled *The Age of Anxiety*, which almost made anxiety a fashionable thing. But this anxiety has its roots in the thought of man's mortality coupled with meaninglessness. This anxiety is a fear or dread of the nothingness of human existence.

For the existentialist, anguish is the underlying, all-pervasive condition of human existence. Those who espouse this view of life reject ideas such as happiness, a sense of well-being, and serenity as naive and foolish ways of denying the despairing tragic aspect of human existence. Jean Paul-Sartre, the French existentialist philosopher, filled a book with this sense of anxiety and titled it *Nausea*, which sums up how you will feel if you ever read it.

In an attempt to run away from such anxiety, to avoid facing our own mortality, the existentialist runs into alienation from everything but himself. Everything else in life is the big "other" so much so that a sense of alienation from everything and everyone else permeates one's life. Talk about loneliness and aloneness and isolation!

Another theme of existentialism is the absurdity of existence. We exist but why now? Why here? Why at all?

A fourth theme to the philosophy of despair is nothingness. As one person put it, "I live then without anything to structure my being and my world, and I am looking into emptiness and the void, hovering over the abyss in fear and trembling and living the life of dread" (Levine 1984, p. 331). This is a pit far more fearful than anything over which Jonathan Edwards ever dangled people.

In the philosophy of despair, death is the final nothingness. Ernest Hemmingway caught the essence of this drab sense of life through one of his characters:

> Some live in it and never felt it but he knew it all was nada y pues nada y nada y pues nada. Our nada who art in nada, nada be thy name thy kingdom nada thy will be nada in nada as it is in nada. Give us this nada our daily nada and nada us our nada as we nada our nadas and nada us not

into nada but deliver us from nada; pues nada. Hail nothing full of nothing, nothing is with thee" (Hemmingway 1987, p. 291). Nada is Spanish for "nothing."

> Unbelief tends to bind man's thought with reference to whether life has meaning and destiny other than dust. Some will not give these things serious thought lest they learn something which may demand a radical change in their lives. There are others who are afraid of the tidal wave of disillusionment and futility which would sweep over their lives if they really faced their own philosophy which teaches that life is without lasting meaning or purpose. Unbelief tends to inhibit, discourage, or demoralize thought with reference to the basic questions of God, man, duty, and destiny. —James D. Bales

MEANING

I began this book asking questions concerning purpose and we end it with questions concerning meaning. The Book of Ecclesiastes touches on a number of existentialist themes. Solomon addresses the apparent monotony, repetition, and meaninglessness of life (1:1-11). He recognizes that death comes to men as well as animals (man has no pre-eminence over the beast). There is oppression in the world (4:1-3). Life is filled with loneliness (4:7-16). Riches are kept by their owner for seeming profit, but to his own hurt (3:13-16). Men work for food and eat, but are not satisfied (6:7-9). All alike perish: man and beast, rich and poor, wise and foolish (9:2-6). How do we make any sense out of life if this is the case?

Solomon had what it took to find the answer: money, time, and wisdom.

From the "under the sun" perspective, life is filled with vanity and striving after the wind, of weariness (1:8; 12:12), of sore travail (1:13; 4:8), of grief and sorrow (1:18; 2:23), of no profit (2:11), of despair (2:20), and is a sore vexation (5:17). Solomon's quest is revealed by the questions he asked in the book:

- For what has man for all his labor, and for the striving of his heart with which he has toiled under the sun? (2:22; 3:9)

- I searched in my heart how to gratify my flesh with wine, while guiding my heart with wisdom, and how to lay hold on folly, till I might see what was good for the sons of men to do under heaven all the days of their lives (2:3).

- For who knows what is good for man in life, all the days of his vain life which he passes like a shadow? Who can tell a man what will happen after him under the sun? (6:12).

- Who is like a wise man? And who knows the interpretation of a thing? (8:1).

Solomon was looking for things worthwhile (2:3), fulfilling (6:3), beautiful (3:11), satisfactory (4:8; 5:10f), enjoyable (2:24-26), and joy (8:15).

He sought these great goods through four avenues, all of which led to dead ends. Did he find what was worthwhile in human wisdom? Perhaps the worthwhile is to be found in pleasure and wealth? Or achievements that survive death? Or profit in work?

His first conclusion was that it all was a striving after the wind and vanity. In fact, it led him to confess, "I hated life, because the work that is wrought under the sun was grievous unto me; for all is vanity and a striving after the wind."

But His more mature conclusion was that the purpose of life could not be found in any one of the goods in the world, but in a life centered in God. Consider:

> I know that whatever God does,
> It shall be forever.
> Nothing can be added to it,
> And nothing taken from it.
> God does it, that men should fear before Him (3:14)

> For in the multitude of dreams and many words there is also vanity. But fear God (5:7).

> It is good that you grasp this,
> And also not remove your hand from the other
> For he who fears God will escape them all (7:18).

> Let us hear the conclusion of the whole matter:
> Fear God and keep His commandments,
> For this is the whole duty of man.
> For God will bring every work into judgment,
> Including every secret thing,
> Whether it is good or whether it is evil (12:13-14).

Some of the philosophers of despair ended their lives as schizophrenics or mad men. They refused the counsel that comes from God's word in their pursuit of truth. You cannot reject your knowledge of God without experiencing adverse consequences. Men like Nietzsche and Sartre lived much of their lives in abject rebellion against God, consequently they lived their lives without attaching meaning to them. What a dismal and nightmarish existence that must be!

I urge you to reject all false philosophies and to begin attaching meaning to your lives and to the trials and temptations you face. Be careful to attach only the meaning God ascribes to them. I urge you to begin facing life from God's perspective, making it your goal to glorify Him. With that commitment in mind, I believe you will be on you way to overcoming whatever sin may be plaguing you, and you will be far better equipped to cope with whatever life presents to you, both good and bad.

All men seek happiness. Some believe happiness means escaping all trials and temptations. I once believed that if I just lived right I would somehow avoid all the troubles of life. This is not true. It simply means that we will avoid many of the unnecessary troubles we bring upon ourselves, and that we will learn to cope effectively with what does come our way.

In order to cope effectively we must acknowledge that the trials and temptations of life have a value beyond the trials and temptations themselves.

MEANING WORKSHEET

Some in the psychological society have trivialized real spiritual problems by reducing them to mere diseases. In so doing, they rob our everyday struggles of any dignity or value.

The existence of God is crucial to our understanding of the value of difficulty. With God in the picture there is a reason to live, to struggle, and even to die. Without God in the picture we may as well eat and drink for tomorrow we die (1 Corinthians 15:32).

Mortimer Adler has rightly concluded,

> More consequences for thought and action follow from the affirmation or denial of God than from answering any other basic question.

183

1. What does Mr. Adler mean by this?

2. How is our thinking and behavior affected by a denial of God's existence?

3. How is our thinking and behavior affected by an affirmation of God's existence?

4. Can man's intellect go unscathed when he denies God's existence?

   a. Romans 1:21-23

   b. Isaiah 45:16-17

THINK ABOUT IT

1. Read James 1:2-4

   a. How do trials test our faith?

   b. What benefits can be derived from the trials of life? (i.e. character, endurance)

   c. How does the reality of death relate to meaning in life?

2. Read 2 Corinthians 4:7-18; Romans 8:18

   a. How can we learn to view the trials of life as light and momentary?

3. What dangers can you see in treating spiritual problems as pathologies (diseases): (i.e., loss of accountability)

   a. What examples can you list where this has occurred in our society (that is, spiritual problems have been reduced to a disease)?

4. Why should the philosophy of despair be rejected?

5. What problems do you face and what ultimate good can you envision coming from them?

READ AND MEDITATE

1. The Book of Ecclesiastes

WORKS SITED

Adler, Mortimer J. 1988. *Great Books of the Western World*, Vol. 2, Encyclopedia Britannica

_____ 1977. *Philosopher at Large*, MacMillan Publishing Co.

Aristotle. 1988. *Great Books of the Western World*, Vol 9, Encyclopedia Britannica

Bales, James D. 1948. *Roots of Unbelief*, The Old Paths Book Club

Barrett, William. *Men of Ideas*, Beattie, M. Codependent No More,

Bobgan, Martin & Deidre. 1985. *How to Counsel from Scripture*, Moody Press

Bradshaw, J. 1988. *Healing the Shame that Binds You*, Health Communications, Inc.

Colson, Charles. 1999. *How Now Shall We Live?* Tyndale

Cottrell, Jack. 1987. *What the Bible Says about God the Redeemer*, College Press

Gross, Martin. 1978. *The Psychological Society*, Random House

Hemmingway, Ernest. 1987. *Complete Works of E. Hemmingway*, Scribners

Horton, Michael. 1992. *Power Religion: The Selling Out of the Evangelical Church?*, Moody Press

Levine, T. Z. 1984. *From Socrates to Sartre: The Philosophic Quest*, Bantam Books

Lewis, C. S. 2001. *Mere Christianity*, HarperSanFranscisco

McClish, Dub. 1983. *Studies in Hebrews*, Valid Publications

McCord, Hugo. 1956. *Happiness Guaranteed*, DeHoff Publications.

McGarvey, J. W. 1975. *McGarvey's Sermons*, Gospel Light Publishing Company

McGuiggan, Jim. 1982. *Romans*, Montex Publishing Co

Milligan, Robert. 1966. *A Brief Treatise on Prayer*, Quality Printing Co

Packer, J. I. 1973. *Knowing God*, InterVarsity Press

Ryken, Leland. 1992. *Words of Delight*, Baker Book House

Made in the USA
Monee, IL
10 February 2024

52745309R00121